THE COMMUNION
OF
LOVE

MATTHEW THE POOR

THE COMMUNION
OF
LOVE

Introduction
by
HENRI NOUWEN

ST. VLADIMIR'S SEMINARY PRESS
CRESTWOOD, NEW YORK 10707
1984

Library of Congress Cataloging in Publication Data

Mattá al-Miskin, 1920-
The communion of love / Matthew the Poor.

1. Spiritual life—Coptic authors.   2. Coptic
Church—Doctrines.   I. Title.
BX136.2.M368   1984   230'.17   84-10561
ISBN 0-88141-036-5

THE COMMUNION OF LOVE

© Copyright 1984

by

ST. VLADIMIR'S SEMINARY PRESS

ISBN 0-88141-036-5

PRINTED IN THE UNITED STATES OF AMERICA
BY
ATHENS PRINTING COMPANY
New York, NY 10018

"Our communion is with the Father and with His Son Jesus Christ."

1 Jn. 1:3

"As Christians, we feel this communion in our depths, the communion of love and life with the Father and the Son by the Holy Spirit."

Fr. Matthew the Poor
Pentecost: The Promise of the Father

Contents

Introduction   9

Preface   13

1. How to Read the Bible   15
2. Christ of the Old and New Testaments   39
3. The Christ of History: A Living Christ   53
4. The Hidden Aspect of the Nativity   65
5. The Righteousness of Humility   79
6. Repentance and Asceticism in the Gospel   85
7. Repentance   91
8. The Deep Meaning of Fasting   109
9. Gethsemane and the Problem of Suffering   123
10. The Passion of Jesus Christ in our Life   131
11. Resurrection and Redemption in the Orthodox Concept   143
12. Between the Resurrection and the Ascension   153
13. The Ascension of Christ   161
14. Pentecost: The Promise of the Father   167
15. The Holy Spirit in Dogmatic Theology and in Ascetic Theology   179
16. The Holy Spirit in the Conflict Between the Enemy and the Kingdom of God   185
17. The Assumption of the Body of the Virgin Mary   199
18. The Virgin in the Theology of the Church   205
19. One Christ and One Catholic Church   215
20. Christian Unity   223

Foreword

It is a pure joy for me to be asked to write a few words about the importance of the spiritual reflections of Father Matta El-Meskeen (Matthew the Poor Man). My joy comes from the deep conviction that we of the Western world must listen to this penetrating message coming to us from the Egyptian desert.

After reading this book, I realized that Father Matta's radical God-centeredness stands in contradiction to our pervasive human-centeredness. All that Father Matta says is guided by the question: "How do I make God the center of my life?" God is the core of every word in this text. That might seem quite "normal" when stated abstractly. Yet these God-centered reflections deeply challenge us who continue to place our own preoccupations and concerns in the center. Over and over again we find ourselves trapped in questions such as: "How does this help me?", "How useful is this for me?", "How does this strike me?", "What can I do with this idea?" All these very acceptable and legitimate questions can easily become ways to avoid facing the truth that God is before we were, and that God and not our needs, desires, hopes, and expectations must be the guide of our thinking, speaking and acting. In our society—with its emphasis on the personal and interpersonal and its interest in emotions, passions, and feelings—Father Matta's radical God-centeredness comes as a shock which wakes us up from a long dream.

For a long time we have been trying to find answers without questioning the validity of the questions. But can we expect right answers to wrong questions? Our first task is to find the right questions. Father Matta is a superb guide in this search for the right questions. The right questions are God's questions to us. When Father Matta reflects on how to read the Bible, about Christ in the Old and New Testaments, about righteousness and humility, about suffering, repentance and fasting, about the resurrection and ascension of Christ and Pentecost, and about Mary, the Church and Christian unity, he brings us back again and again to theology, that is, to raising questions from the divine perspective.

In his first chapter, Father Matta states it clearly: "Although it may appear outwardly that we may make our way towards God, the joyful and wonderful truth is that it is God who comes to us, as a lover and a deeply loving Father." Throughout his reflections Father Matta holds on to this "joyful truth." When he speaks of Christian unity he writes: "To seek unity before arriving at a state of complete abandonment of heart and soul and mind to God is to enter into either an emotional conflict, so that we seek unity for our own sake, or else into an intellectual illusion—seeking unity as an exigency which the logic of faith necessitates." Thus it is again God, not ourselves, to whom Father Matta draws the eyes of our hearts and minds.

Does that mean that people do not count? On the contrary! Father Matta is a very perceptive observer of human behavior. He knows what goes on in the human heart. He speaks about it with great compassion. But he never hesitates to say that any search for inner or outer peace outside of God is doomed to fail. "Union," he writes, ". . . is to encounter each other in the presence of God and not just in the presence of one another."

When I try to express the impact of Father Matta's spiritual writings upon me, I would say that he helps me to "discover the true space." Father Matta has evoked for me that "objective" divine space in which I can freely walk, raise the right questions concerning God's Love, and search for answers that gradually grow in me as I dwell in that holy space. These writings pull me out of my subjective rumination and introspection and lead me into a new and open space where God dwells and invites me to dwell with him.

The awareness that this book will offer that divine space to many of my brothers and sisters in Christ fills me with great joy and gratitude.

—Henri J.M. Nouwen

Preface

"Behold, the Lord is riding on a swift
cloud and comes to Egypt."
Is. 19:1

"In that day there will be an altar to the
Lord in the midst of the land of Egypt,
and a pillar to the Lord at its borders. It
will be a sign and a witness to the Lord
of hosts in the land of Egypt."
Is. 19:19,20

"Blessed be Egypt My people."
Is. 19:25

Father Matta El-Meskeen (Matthew the Poor Man)
belongs to the Coptic (Egyptian) Orthodox Church. He is
the spiritual father in the Monastery of St. Macarius in the
desert of Scetis (Scete), Wadi El-Natroon.

Fr. Matta was born in 1919. In 1948 he abandoned his
professional occupation as a pharmacist and entered the
Monastery of St. Samuel the Confessor (7th cent.) south
of Fayoum. For the next 20 years he lived as a hermit in
various locations, either in the vicinity of a monastery or in
complete solitude in the depth of the desert.

Very early in his monastic life he was joined by several
young educated people who had met him previously during
his lecturing at various religious seminars. These monks
formed the nucleus of the present community of the Monastery of St. Macarius.

In 1969, at the request of the late Patriarch Cyrill VI,
Fr. Matta and his disciples left their caves in the Wadi
Rayan desert, where they had pursued their monastic voca-
tion for ten years, and moved to Scete. Here they built anew

13

the whole monastery complex, extending and modernizing it considerably. The present community consists of about 100 monks.

His first book, *The Orthodox Life in Prayer,* Fr. Matta published in 1951. Today he is the author of more than 50 major works and hundreds of articles and sermons that regularly appear in the monthly review *St. Mark* published by the Monastery.

The readers of *The Communion of Love* will note that the writings of Fr. Matta proceed from a dogmatic understanding of the Church as revealed in the depth of his personal mystical experience. Moreover, most of the articles present his recorded sermons and talks, thus bearing a hallmark of direct inspiration. Father Matta acknowledges that he never personally re-reads what he writes or what others have recorded from his talks, and does not remember its content. Hence every new article is the result of fresh inspiration. This is why different articles deal with the same subject in different aspects, making them individually unique, yet complimentary.

The present collection of articles is the first of this kind in the English language and includes only a portion of the translated works of Fr. Matta. Several articles have been translated from English into Russian, French, German, Italian, and Japanese.

The articles in this collection are organized by subject in an ascending order, starting with Old Testament prophesies about Jesus Christ, through spiritual exposition of the Church's teaching on the mystery of salvation, to the present searchings of the Church. Also included are two articles about the Mother of God, who is the personified image of the Church.

Written by a mystic of profound spirituality, these articles are marked by a simple, practical approach and can be of benefit to Christians on any spiritual level.

Julian the Alien

1.

How to Read the Bible

The Bible in relation to the reader

The Bible is different from all other books. Other books are written by people; the Bible, however, not only contains the sayings and commandments of God but was also written entirely under His divine inspiration. So we might say that it is God's book that was given to us to lead us into everlasting life.

Although the dialogue, events, history, and stories in the Old and New Testaments center on man, it is in fact God who is veiled in them, for the Bible describes God and reveals Him through events. Yet we were not given a complete picture in one generation, or one book, or even over the whole extended period; it is with great difficulty that the Bible struggles to give us a simplified mental image of God by relating His direct dealings with His people over a period of five thousand years. This is so that no one in any age need be deprived of perceiving something about God that will satisfy a need, so much so that each one experiences such a flood of joy that he believes he has come to know God and completely comprehended Him. But whoever has the intellectual audacity to try to supercede his human limitations by searching within himself to perceive a perfect image of God is doomed to failure and loses the ability to attain even the small things appropriate to his stature.

It is immeasurably difficult for us to comprehend God, whose days have neither beginning nor end, for He is perfect and, while it is true that we may pereceive Him, His perfection is unfathomable, and so it is with all His works.

As well as revealing God and introducing Him to us, the Bible tries in many ways to prepare us inwardly to receive Him. Although it may appear outwardly that we make our way toward God, the joyful and wonderful truth is that it is God who comes to us, as a lover and deeply loving father. "If any man loves me, he will keep my word, and my Father will love him and we will come and make our home with him" (Jn. 14:23). This is why the Lord commands us to prepare our hearts for His blessed coming. "My heart is steadfast, O God. My heart is steadfast" (Ps. 57:7).

So we see that the Bible as a whole reveals God mysteriously and prepares us to receive Him in our hearts, that we may live with Him from this moment on as a preparation for what will be at the end of time, when God will be revealed openly and we shall meet Him face to face to live with Him forever.

The reader in relation to the Bible

There are two ways of reading:

The first is when a man reads and puts himself and his mind in control of the text, trying to subject its meaning to his own understanding and then comparing it with the understanding of others.

The second is when a man puts the text on a level above himself and tries to bring his mind into submission to its meaning, and even sets the text up as a judge over him, counting it as the highest criterion.

The first way is suitable for any book in the world, whether it be a work of science or of literature. The second is indispensable in reading the Bible. The first way gives man mastery over the world, which is his natural role. The second gives God mastery as the all-wise and all-powerful Creator.

But if man confuses the roles of these two methods, he stands to lose from them both, for if he reads science and literature as he should read the Gospel, he grows small in stature, his academic ability diminishes, and his dignity among the rest of creation dwindles.

And if he reads the Bible as he should read science, he understands and feels God to be small; the divine being appears limited and His awesomeness fades. We acquire a false sense of our own superiority over divine things—the very same forbidden thing that Adam committed in the beginning.

Spiritual understanding and intellectual memorization

Thus in reading the Bible we aim at understanding and not at research, investigation, or study, for the Bible is to be understood, not investigated. It is therefore appropriate here to point to the difference between spiritual understanding and intellectual memorization.

Spiritual understanding centers on the acceptance of a divine truth, which gradually reveals itself, rising on the horizon of the mind till it pervades all. If the mind and its reactions are brought into willing obedience to that truth, the divine truth continues to permeate the mind even more and the mind develops with it endlessly. "To know the love of Christ which surpasses knowledge, that you may be filled with all the fullness of God" (Eph. 3:19). It is clear from this verse that the knowledge and love of God and divine things in general are immeasurably above the level of knowledge, that is human knowledge. It is therefore futile and foolish for us to try to "investigate" the things of God in an attempt to grasp them and make them yield to our intellectual powers.

On the contrary, it is we who must yield to the love of God so that our minds may be open to the divine truth. It is then that we will be prepared to receive surpassing knowledge. That "being rooted and grounded in love, [you] may have power to comprehend with all the saints what is the breadth and length and height and depth" (Eph. 3:17,18).

Intellectual memorization demands that we pass from a state of submission to the truth (through understanding) to a state of mastery over it and possession of it. It requires that the mind progress step by step through investigation until it is on a level with the truth, then little by little rise above it until it can control it, recalling it and repeating it at will as if the truth were a possession and the mind its owner.

Thus, memorization is a matter of determining the truth, summing it up, and defining it as closely as possible, so that the mind may absorb it and store it away. Thus, intellectual memorization is the reverse of spiritual understanding, for spiritual understanding expands with the knowledge of the truth, and the truth, in its turn, opens up into "all the fullness of God" (Eph. 3:19), to infinity. Intellectual memorization therefore weakens divine truth, and strips it of its power and breadth, so it is not a suitable way of approach to the Bible, and brings minimal results.

Spiritual memorization

There is another way of memorizing the word of God, by which we may recall and review the text, though not whenever and however we wish, but rather whenever and however God wishes. This is spiritual, not intellectual, memorization, and God grants it by His Spirit to those who understand His words, "The Counselor, the Holy Spirit, whom the Father will send in my name, will teach you all things and bring to your remembrance all that I have said to you" (Jn. 14:26).

Just as God gives spiritual understanding to those who ask sincerely and honestly to know Him, at which their minds are opened to understand the text (cf. Lk. 24:45), so also is spiritual memorization a spiritual work that God gives to those who have been granted to be witnesses for Him. When the Holy Spirit recalls certain words to us, He does so in depth and breadth, not simply reminding us of the text of a verse, but giving with it irresistible wisdom and spiritual power to bring out the glory of the verse and the power of

God in it. A spirit of censure is also sent with the words to prick the heart.[1]

Thus there is a striking difference between intellectual memorization by rote and recollection through the Holy Spirit.

Nevertheless, we must be prepared for this spiritual recollection by keeping our hearts conscious of the word of God through pondering upon it frequently and storing it up in our hearts out of love and delight. "Thy words were found, and I ate them" (Jr. 15:16) and they were "sweeter than honey to my mouth" (Ps. 119:103). We can constantly recite to ourselves: "on His law he meditates day and night" (Ps. 1:2), and every time we come across a profitable word we can impress it on our hearts: "I have laid up thy words in my heart, that I may not sin against Thee" (Ps. 119:11), just as God warns us to talk of them "when you sit in your house, and when you walk by the way, and when you lie down, and when you rise. And you shall bind them as a sign upon your hand, and they shall be as frontlets between your eyes" (Dt. 6:7,8).

Now there is a great difference between a man who recites and meditates on the word of God because it is sweet and beneficial to his soul and rejoices his heart and comforts his spirit, and one who meditates on it in order to repeat it to other people so that he can stand out as a teacher and skillful servant of the Gospel. For the first, the word remains, for it builds an awareness of heart or a relationship with God; for the second it simply passes into the intellectual memory where he can use it to build relationships with people!

So if a man tries to read the Bible and memorize verses to

[1]The meaning of this phrase can be explained this way: The revelation of the spiritual meaning of the word of God, as a truth, endowes us with a supreme gift of spiritual richness and deifies us through His participation in the truth. At the same time, however, in the light of divine truth the awareness of our creational limitations and inadequacy rise before us with special acuteness, because the spirit of grace is not only the spirit of glory and wisdom but also the spirit of humility, reflecting the humility of God. In the presence of God's greatness we involuntarily see, as in a mirror, our own insignificance, which in the light of the truth stands out with uncontestable obviousness, and tenderness sweetly pricks the heart prompting it to advance in perfection.

use them to teach people and give a spoken witness, before submitting himself to the divine truth and acting according to it and opening his mind to receive spiritual understanding, he only gains knowledge and does not give a fruitful witness, no matter how many verses or orderly proofs he may present with great intellectual skill, for the Spirit will have left him. The worst use we can make of the Bible is to use it simply as a source of proof verses.

Spiritual understanding of the sayings, commandments, and teachings of God is our entrance into the mystery of the Gospel: "To you it has been given to know the secrets of the Kingdom of God" (Lk. 8:10). And the sign of spiritual understanding is our sense that there is within us an inexhaustible spring of spiritual insights into the word of God, and that each truth is related to all the rest. In our hearts we are able to relate every verse we read to another verse and every insight broadens into harmony with another, so that the Gospel easily becomes a unified whole.

This position is not attained only by those who have spent long years reading the Bible. It may be that someone who has only a few months' experience with it may be given this sense, so that using the few verses he is familiar with he is able to speak zealously of God with a sincerity and power that attract the hearts of others to God. For such a man it is enough to read a verse once for it to be indelibly imprinted on his heart forever, for the word of God is spiritual; it is even in some sense a spirit, as the Lord says: "The words that I have spoken to you are spirit and life" (Jn. 6:63).

A practical introduction to understanding the Gospel

There is no intellectual means of entering into the Gospel, for the Gospel is spiritual. It must be obeyed and lived through the Spirit before it can be understood. If anyone living outside the Gospel tries to understand it he will stumble and fall, and if he dares to try to teach it, he will be a stumbling block to those who follow him. But if anyone has true zeal, burning love, and total obedience to God and carries out just one of the commandments of the Gospel precisely, that person enters into the mystery of the Gospel without being aware of it.

The first thing we discover is God's faithfulness in fulfilling His promises in our own souls. This makes our minds eager to receive the spark of living faith that settles in the heart and kindles there a great fire of love and fear of God. Spiritual experience increases and the level of understanding of the Gospel deepens according to the degree to which we carry out its commandments faithfully and precisely.

A sincere and humble acceptance of obedience to God that springs from a heart undefiled by falsehood, hypocrisy, love of display, or exhibitionism, and not looking for any particular results, may be considered the beginning of the true way to the knowledge of God. This is because intentions are tested by temptations as we try to carry out the commandments; we are helped according to the degree of our faith and perseverance, and in so far as we receive help, our trust increases and our knowledge of God and His ways grows surer.

All this is to say that the spiritual understanding of the Gospel and of God is the result of the formation of a relationship with God through obedience to His commandments. This is not simply an understanding of texts and verses, but an understanding of the power of the word and knowledge of the life that springs from the verse based on experience, trust, evidence, and an unshakable faith in God.

A fine example of reading and understanding the Gospel

The greatest commandment by which we may experience the providence of God, and by obedience to which we may obtain spiritual power which unveils to us the mysteries and secrets of the Bible and lights the way ahead, is that we should leave everything and follow Christ. For this commandment sums up the whole Gospel! This is the verse that St. Antony heard. It touched him deeply, and he carried it out with precise determination. Through doing so he attained a life that was in accordance with the Gospel, and understanding, knowledge, and recollection of the Bible that astonished the scholars and theologians, as we know from St. Athanasius the Great. And all this in spite of the fact that St. Antony could neither read nor write.

Many of the Fathers followed the same pattern and the same marvels took place in them, for they attained the heights of knowledge of the Bible, of God, and spiritual direction, though they themselves were illiterate. Among them were the great ascetics Pambo and Paphnutius, the diciple of Macarius the Great, of whom Palladius says that he had the grace of the knowledge of the holy books and was an able expositor, though he could not read or write.

Many others in the world, both men and women, educated and uneducated, have entered into the mystery of the Gospel through one of the many commandments, such as voluntary poverty and simplicity of life, refusing to set money aside for emergencies and putting their faith in God before all other considerations. Through this they have tasted the wonders of God, their minds have been opened, they have perceived the mystery of the divine plan and understood God's words as people who lived them out in experience and fulfilled them. In this way they were able to evangelize with great faith and courage. Others have also entered into the rejection of worldly pleasures and lifeless pastimes. They have experienced the power of the word of God and found in it great comfort and delight. They have understood how a man lives by the word more than by food and medicine; they have known God and tasted Him and their minds have been illumined by His words.

Yet others have entered into the mystery of the Gospel through secret acts of sacrifice, giving their money, energy, or time to serve the poor, the deprived, the afflicted, and those bowed down by various tragedies. They have acted in silent courage, giving all they possess, bearing all they are able. Such as these have acquired knowledge, perception, and understanding of the Gospel and the commandments of the Lord, but not the understanding that comes from meditating on the beauty of the words and the exposition of their meaning. It is rather the understanding that springs from experience and is transformed into eternal life, forming a living relationship with Christ.

Academic meditation and practical meditation

There is an academic understanding of meditation on the Bible and a practical understanding of it.

Academic meditation is the product of ideas resulting from study, research, pondering the meanings of the verses and their relation to each other, and arriving at facts by a process of logical deduction.

Practical meditation comes through inspiration, which the soul perceives as a result of its experience and its trials and struggles with the truth when it follows the comandments of the Gospel. This is also supplemented by the illuminations and promptings of the Spirit, which we receive in due time without having previously acquired knowledge of the things revealed.

Academic meditation on the Bible stimulates the mind but leaves the spirit unmoved. It makes the listener desire the truth without showing him how to enter into it. It provides us with an image of God but cannot bring us face to face with Him. Academic meditation alone, though useful in itself, without practical implementation leads to a worship that is merely formal and to a false intellectual devotion to the Gospel. "This people honors me with their lips, but their heart is far from me" (Mk. 7:6).

Regrettable as it is, this type of reading, understanding, exposition, and teaching of the Bible has precedence in our Church and indeed throughout the world at the present time. The Gospel has been reduced to a source from which one may quote verses or prove principles, and the ideas it contains have become academic points to support sermons and articles. So the Gospel has become a reliable way of gaining fame, academic degrees, and the admiration of the world, though the basis of the Gospel and the truth it contains is the enemy of fame and false worldly knowledge, and the enemy of the admiration of the world. The Church thus suffers a great loss when it abandons the practical teaching of the Bible and is concerned with the academic.

As for practical meditation on the Bible, it is attained by receiving divine truth through secret obedience to the commandments, and as a result the heart faithfully clings to God in seemly fear and true humility. This builds a practical and sure relationship with God.

That is to say that practical meditation builds an inner life with God that impregnates a person's words, thoughts, and teachings with divine power. Thus with a single word he may convey truth to a listener, as did the Fathers, who lived the Gospel with all their heart, mind, and power. Their words were not eloquent or full of high-flown meditations, but they conveyed the mystery since they had the power to give new life to the listener.

In the sayings of the ascetic Fathers of the fourth century and later, this was the normal pattern of instruction: A novice would go to the old Father and say, "Speak to me a word that I may live." The old man would say very little to him, but because of the power of his experience and the grace it brought, this little would be enough for the novice to live by and overcome all the difficulties he faced. This is the truest picture there is of how the Gospel should be understood and preached. How appropriate for us today are the words of the Apostle: "If you know these things, blessed are you if you do them" (Jn. 13:17).

The power of a life of practical simplicity

If we look back to the early days of the Church, we are astonished at its power, especially that of the newly-founded Churches. In spite of the fact that the people were simple and ignorant of the Bible—for manuscripts were only rarely possessed by individuals—and in spite of the newness of their faith in Christ and the deep influence of their old pagan customs, their spiritual life and their demonstrations of faith, love, and zeal were fine examples of a powerful life lived according to the precepts of the Gospel, a model for practical understanding of the meaning of eternal life, the Kingdom of God, living by faith, dying to the world, faithfulness to Christ, expectation of His second coming, and faith in the resurrection. Even up to the present time, we still draw on their faith and tradition, and understand only with difficulty the letters that were written to them, which they understood easily and lived out.

The secret of all this is that they lived by what they heard. Every commandment fell on faithful hearts prepared to act sincerely. All the words of Christ entered deeply into the fabric of daily life. The Gospel was translated into work and life.

Those simple people understood the Gospel. They understood that it was a life to be lived, not principles to be discussed, and they refused to understand it on a purely academic level. Up to this day, faithful followers of Christ still draw life for themselves from the living spring of the understanding of those early Christians.

These early communities, burning with love for Christ, had no creeds, no patrology, no expositions of Scripture, but the few words of Christ that reached their ears immediately became their creed, needing no explanations or teaching or interpretation, but needing, as they saw it, to be experienced and lived. Through experience they would discover the power of the words and bring to light the mysteries they contained. And so their zeal and love and faith in Christ and the Gospel would grow.

When they heard "Blessed are the poor in spirit," they sold everything and laid their money at the feet of the apostles.

When they heard "Blessed are those who mourn now," they despised all suffering and weariness in the service of the Lord.

When they heard "Blessed are those who are persecuted for righteousness' sake," they bore the cruelest humiliations and insults and attacks.

When they heard "Watch and pray," they met in the catacombs to watch and pray all night.

When they heard "Love your enemies," history recorded

no resistance put up by the Christians, whether positive or negative, against their persecutors. And they bowed their necks to the sword in humility and obedience to honor the words of Christ.

This was for them the meaning of reading the Gospel and understanding it. There was born in them a hunger and thirst for the righteousness of God, and this is why the Holy Spirit was at His most active in working with them. He would give power to the word, strengthen their hearts, support them in weakness, lead them in the darkness, comfort them in distress, and accompany them along the way till they gave up their spirit into the hand of its Creator with great glory.

Reading with and without practical application

Reading remains useless, understanding powerless, and memorization a mere repetition of empty words, unless we obey the commandment and the word becomes a law of life, no matter what sacrifice, cost, hardship, or scorn we may bear. And the Lord Jesus says even more than this; He says that whoever reads His words and understands them but does not obey them will suffer destruction and great loss, like a man who builds his house on the sand. "And every one who hears these words of mine and does not do them will be like a foolish man who built his house upon the sand; and the rain fell, and the floods came, and the winds blew and beat against that house, and it fell; and great was the fall of it" (Mt. 7:26,27).

Perhaps you may say, with me, that it would have been better if he had never built, or heard or known or learned, anything.

The life of the Pharisees and Sadducees was like this: minute obedience to the law, skilled explanations and expositions of the commandments, legal opinions so detailed that they went beyond the truth and simplicity of the Spirit, dead works and a life that was spiritually desolate. "And behold, a lawyer stood up to put Him to the test, saying, 'Teacher, what shall I do to inherit eternal life?' He said to him, 'What

is written in the law? How do you read?' And he answered,
'You shall love the Lord your God with all your heart, and
with all your soul, and with all your strength, and with all
your mind; and your neighbor as yourself.' And He said to
him, 'You have answered right; do this and you will live"
(Lk. 10:25-28).

The Lord compares those who hear the word and obey
it with those who built houses on the rock. This points to the
fact that the power of the word is dependent entirely on one's
practical experience of it (for one can only receive and know
help in difficulty and danger), the mysterious aid of the Holy
Spirit, and sincere obedience to the precepts of the Gospel.
A word on a man's lips, if he truly lives by it, is like a house
built on a rock; it is firm and has nothing to fear. "Everyone
then who hears these words of mine and does them will be
like a wise man who built his house upon the rock; and the
rain fell, and the floods came, and the winds blew and beat
upon that house, but it did not fall, because it had been
founded on the rock" (Mt. 7:24,25). And here perhaps you
may say with me, "If only my house could be built on the
rock, and my reading and understanding and knowledge of
the Gospel be used for living, rather than as a subject for
talking, preaching, conversation, and meditation."

A grievous example of great knowledge without action

Balaam was a man of vision who could see into the future
and had prophetic powers, so he would hear and speak of the
great works of God. But he was rejected and became a terrifying warning, and an example of those who speak the word
of God, who are able to reveal mysteries and give true
prophecies, who pronounce blessings and offer sacrifices, like
Balaam, while their hearts are unclean, secretly living far
from God. Listen to what he says of himself: "The oracle of
Balaam the son of Beor, the oracle of the man whose eye is
opened, the oracle of him who hears the words of God, and
knows the knowledge of the Most High, who sees the vision
of the Almighty, falling down, but having his eyes uncovered"

(Num. 24:15,16). But all these gifts were not enough to
turn Balaam's heart away from a life of evil. Balaam fell into
grave error, according to the Holy Apostles, Jude in his
epistle, Peter in his second epistle, and John in the Book of
Revelation. Even though outwardly he blessed the people of
God, he was secretly working against them by wicked con-
sultation and was pleased to receive a reward for that sin.

Balaam attained the highest level of knowledge, understanding, vision, and prophecy accessible to a spiritual man,
but his behavior was no better than that of the most evil and
deceitful of men. His story clearly shows that the understanding and teaching of spiritual matters, even to the level of
prophecy, if not supported by a holy life and conduct, in
integrity and the fear of God, cannot save us from the curse
and death that set the seal on the life of Balaam.

"Take heed how you hear"

Before you read the Bible or hear the word of God, look
within yourself to see where the word of God will come to
rest. Here we go back to the well-loved parable of the sower:

> The ones along the path are those who have heard;
> then the devil comes and takes away the word from
> their hearts, that they may not believe and be saved.
> And the ones on the rock are those who, when they
> hear the word, receive it with joy; but these have no
> root, they believe for a while and in time of temptation
> fall away. And as for what fell among the thorns,
> they are those who hear, but as they go on their way
> they are choked by the cares and riches and pleasures
> of life, and their fruit does not mature. And as for
> that in the good soil, they are those who, hearing the
> word, hold it fast in an honest and good heart, and
> bring forth fruit with patience. (Lk. 8:12-15)
> Take heed then how you hear. (Lk. 8:18)

When it comes to hearing the Gospel there are four kinds

of listeners. They do not need to be explained or clarified, because the Lord Jesus explained them Himself, so look and see how the Lord says you should hear. Is it with a heart that spends all day along the roadside? Or with a heart that has no depth because it is afraid to sit alone and examine its life? Or with a heart inclined to set aside money as insurance for the future? Or with a heart always loaded with imaginary cares?

Take heed how you hear the Gospel. It seems that the Lord wants to say that we hear with our hearts rather than our ears, and that the inner life affects the word of God, either killing it, or making it live and thrive. So whoever wants to hear the word well, understand it, and hold it fast in an honest and good heart should prepare his heart inwardly so that the word may safely take root there, finding in his heart faithfulness to God and truthfulness in word and promise. It is absolutely impossible that anyone should understand what he hears of the word of God, if he is not completely honest before God and has not determined to surrender his life, his responsibilities, his interests, his money, his future, and his own honor and lay them at God's feet.

For how can anyone who is afraid of the future understand when the Lord says, "Do not be anxious about tomorrow," and "Do not be anxious about your life" (Mt. 6:34, 25)? How can anyone who is concerned about honor understand the cross? How can anyone who is afraid of sickness or death understand the resurrection?

Anyone who asks to read the Gospel is in fact asking for eternal life, and anyone who asks for eternal life has to take a clear stand with regard to the present life!

Forgetting the word is a psychological deception

There is no finer illustration than that of James the Apostle, when he describes the man who hears the word of the Gospel and forgets it as if he had seen his face in a mirror and immediately forgotten what he looked like. For whoever disregards the word he hears, immediately loses his self-perception.

One kind of man listens to the Gospel, receives the word, and stores it up in his heart. He is constantly aware of the instruction he has received and sets it before him like a mirror, using it continuously to correct his speech and thoughts and actions.

Another kind of man listens to the Gospel, but not a single word of what he hears stays in his heart, because it is oblivious and irresponsible, and concerned with matters more important to it than the Gospel and eternal life; they may be his work, his troubles, his pleasures, or concerns that he may consider to be in God's service. Or there may be nothing at all in his heart, and this is also a disaster, for while he is reading the Gospel, he may be so moved that he sighs or even weeps, but afterward he becomes involved in his own affairs and forgets his sighs and tears. A man like this may imagine that his forgetfulness is beyond his own control, but this is a psychological trick. The truth is that the soul wants to forget the Gospel because it does not like it.

One may read the Gospel regularly every day, but feel that there is an unbridgeable gap between what he reads every day and what he does every day. This unbridgeable gap is produced by forgetfulness. As the days go by, reading the Gospel becomes no more powerful or effective, and no change of life, or even progress along the path, takes place.

This forgetfulness is what James the Apostle considers self-deception!

> Receive with meekness the implanted word, which is able to save your souls. But be doers of the word, and not hearers only, deceiving yourselves. For if any-one is a hearer of the word and not a doer, he is like a man who observes his natural face in a mirror; for he observes himself and goes away and at once forgets what he was like. (Jm. 1:21-24)

The uncircumcised ear

This significant spiritual expression was spoken by St. Stephen the martyr to the council set up to judge him, when he felt that they were resisting the Holy Spirit to satisfy their own purposes.

"You stiff-necked people, uncircumcised in heart and ears, you always resist the Holy Spirit" (Ac. 1:51).

The Holy Spirit speaks to us through the Gospel, but only the circumcised ear can hear His voice, that is the ear whose foreskin has been removed; by the foreskin St. Stephen means lack of submission to God and having a heart too far from God to hear His voice. Those who have uncircumcised ears or hearts are strangers among the people of God. They do not understand His commandments or respond to them, because they regard themselves as having no commitment to obey.

Those whose ears are uncircumcised neither hear the Spirit, nor are influenced by Him, nor respond to Him, because on their own will they have refused to put themselves under submission to the Holy Spirit out of fear of Him. They fear that the Spirit may ask them to give up things or positions or principles or relationships, which they find beneficial or pleasurable and important to them personally. To give them up would be a loss they would not want to accept, so they are afraid of the Holy Spirit lest He should ask them to act against themselves or against the world, for their selves are dear to them and the world is their delight. Those who have uncircumcised ears are those who have not cut off the foreskin of their selves and do not want to cut the foreskin of the world from either their hearts or ears. They are not prepared to sacrifice anything ever, or at least they are not prepared to sacrifice everything for God. They hear the Holy Spirit, but pay Him no heed, trying every time to stifle the voice of their conscience. They have from the start excused themselves from the responsibility of listening to the voice of God.

This situation had earlier been described by the Prophet

Isaiah, and the Lord Himself made a revealing comment on it:

> Seeing they do not see, and hearing they do not hear, nor do they understand . . . For this people's heart has grown dull, and their ears are heavy of hearing, and their eyes they have closed, lest they should perceive with their eyes, and hear with their ears, and understand with their heart, and turn for me to heal them. (Mt. 13:13-15; cf. Is. 6:9)

Here the Lord exposes the intention of His hearers. They give the appearance of reading and listening to the commandments of God, but in fact they were determined not to be influenced. So they closed their eyes and ears, so that they should neither see nor hear. The Lord exposed their reason for this: it was that they were afraid lest the voice of God should sound so clear and the censure of the Holy Spirit become so convincing that they would be forced to give up their erroneous positions and their embezzled possessions, the plans they had made for their future, and the sinful relationships for which they had sold their souls, and not only their souls, but also eternal life and even God Himself. They, like many of us, did not refuse to read or hear the Gospel, but when they came to certain passages, certain verses, or certain commandments, they would become confused, pass them over quickly, and close their eyes, escaping anxiously from the voice of the Holy Spirit. This is where the uncircumcised ear shows itself, for it is disturbed by the voice of God and avoids it, just as the snake stops its ears so as not to hear the voice of the magician and obey and submit to it. "O foolish Galatians! Who has bewitched you" (Ga. 3:1) that you should not obey the truth?

Let us stop a while and return together to these passages and verses and commandments that we have deliberately avoided with cowardly determination. Our hearts protest at our obstinacy, and tremble and beat fast and painfully, for we are aware that we are resisting the Holy Spirit and putting ourselves in danger of death and estrangement from God by this deviousness. Let us quickly correct our attitude to the voice of God! Perhaps now is the time to take our self by storm, break its obstinacy and pride, cut off its pleasures and fears and turn to follow the voice of God. "Remember then from what you have fallen, repent and do the works you did at first. If not, I will come to you and remove your lampstand from its place, unless you repent" (Rv. 2:5).

It may be that you are afraid to face your desire for greatness and leadership, or your impurity or your enmity, malice, and hatred toward others who threaten your own interests, or your treachery, or your cruelty, injustice or crooked judgments, or your dishonesty, stealing, wrongful acquisition of goods, creating and love of undeserved gain, or your lying, or your lack of trust in God and reliance on money and insurance for the future, or it may be more than all these, since you are running away with all your being from the face of God. You have no foothold on safe ground and you are trying now to hide your face from Him who sits upon the throne, closing your eyes lest you see! (Cf. Lk. 8:10.) In this situation, reading the Gospel is of no avail, and hearing it only brings judgment.

But the circumcised ear has had ts foreskin removed, and there is no longer a barrier preventing it from hearing the voice of God, like the ear of the young Samuel who lived in purity and humility in the sanctuary: "Speak, [Lord,] for thy servant hears" (1 Sm. 3:10). The ear is open to the authority of the Gospel and joyfully submissive to the voice of God, alert to hear Hs call, ready to respond no matter what may be demanded. Those whose ears are circumcised are very courageous and able to take action against themselves in obedience to the voice of the Almighty. The heart that is ready to accept the great demands of God is able to hear every inflection in the voice of God and does not miss a single word.

If, after all this, you ask, "How can I acquire an ear that can hear the voice of God?" I would answer, "Prepare yourself first to receive His demands and requests and directions, and be ready in your heart to carry them out, no matter what the cost. Immediately you will have an ear that hears the voice of Almighty God!" "Morning by morning he wakens, he wakens my ear to hear as those who are taught. The Lord God has opened my ear, and I was not rebellious" (Is. 50:4,5).

The voice of the Son of God

"Behold, I stand at the door and knock; if anyone hears my voice and opens the door, I will come in to him and eat with him, and he with me" (Rv. 3:20). The Lord does not only knock at the heart's door, He even calls His sheep by name, so that we may hear and open up to let Him into our lives, to share with us the tears of our supper and then to share with us His wedding feast.

We do not need to go in search of God, as if He were in hiding far away; we would simply exhaust ourselves in searching, imagining, meditating, and scrutinizing books. Yet the whole time He is standing before us at the door of our heart, never going away. The knocks at the door are His words. He never stops knocking all the days of our life, so that the spirit may wake from its slumber and distinguish the voice of its lover.

We do not need to resort to fervent pleas and tears and emotional supplications that the Lord may come to us, for He is always present and is knocking even now. He will not stop, because He wants to enter our lives. He finds His own rest with us, and His greatest joy is to share with us our cross and our dark night, for He still loves the cross.

But it is we who do not rightly value His voice, mistakenly making little of it and disdaining it.

Mary Magdalene underwent the same temptation when she sat weepng at the tomb and thought the Lord standing before her was the gardener, so that she kept begging him to give her the body of Jesus that she might wrap it in a shroud. When the Lord lost patience He called her by name and immediately she recognized Him. How often have we stood weeping looking far away up to heaven where we think the Lord Jesus lives! He is present and standing before us, and all that prevents us from encountering Him is our heart's lack of perception! How often have we stood praying before Him, begging Him to speak to us, hoping that we might hear Him, but it was useless! He never stops calling us by name; nothing prevents us from hearing His voice but our preoccupation with our own daily problems.

The mistake we make is that we want to see Him in the midst of the daily events that fill our mental and emotional emptiness. But in fact the Lord is present now beyond all these things, beyond time and events, which He controls according to His own wise plan. The alert and simple soul notices the touch of His hand writing the story of its salvation through the years and the succession of events. Our successes and our failures work together in a positive way guided by the Almighty for our salvation. Temporal losses are not spiritual losses, and trouble, sadness, pain, and sickness are the language of divine providence, its secret code, which when deciphered in the Spirit spells resurrection, joy, and eternal glory.

The other mistake we make is that we want to hear the voice of the Son of God with our physical ear, speaking a human language with the voice of a man! But the voice of the Son of God cannot be so limited. It is a power that moves the soul, raises it up, and refreshes it. It is a deep incomprehensible peace. It is rest and comfort. It is life itself in its limitless breadth and height. So where are the words in which His language and voice may be expressed?

God speaks, and everyone on the face of the earth can hear His voice, understand, and respond, as if he is being called personally by name. His voice is the voice of all the ages; it does not fade or die on the breeze, nor is it restricted or return to Him empty. There will come a time when He will call and the whole of creation will rise from its death.

"If any man hears my voice . . ." But no one can hear the voice of the Son of God except him who is raised in spirit to the level where God can direct and call him, the level of the Kingdom and life with God, that is, the level above daily events. There he can receive from Him instruction for his life and a plan for his salvation through these very daily events, and even through using them. No one can hear the voice of the Son of God except him who opens his heart and mind to understand His language, whose words and tones are made of love, tenderness, peace, kindness, and constant fatherly care, no matter how cruel life and its circumstances may appear to be.

If your ear is spiritually trained to understand the symbols of the divine message as they appear in temporal events, you will hear the Lord's hand knocking at the door as you read the words. He will be knocking at your door, sometimes gently, sometimes hard, and you will hear His voice through the clamor and the storms, as well as through a gentle breeze. He calls you to open the door for Him, to receive from Him the mystery of His wedding feast, after sharing with you the bread of your tears.

The Lord is near. He is humble and His voice is low, lower than the voice of a man, but deep, deeper than eternity itself.

Doing honor to the reading and hearing of the Gospel

The man who is alive to God does not allow the word of the Gospel to slip away from him or be forgotten. Rather, in respect, reverence, and fear he makes it as a crown for his head and sets it over his whole life.

The zeal of the pious is very evident when they listen to the Gospel. They look as if they have entered into the presence of God, or as if they are standing around the altar about to receive the body and blood. It is not that they have simply cultivated the custom of honoring the Gospel or appearing to do so, as the hypocrites do, but rather that they receive from it power upon power, as if they were hearing the voice of God Himself.

All this was very clear in the early Church, and the Church still observes the same zeal, reverence, and veneration at the reading and hearing of the Gospel. The tradition of the Church has preserved certain significant gestures; the priest never reads the Gospel in church before offering a special prayer, so that he and the congregation can be made worthy to hear the Holy Gospel. Befor he begins to read, the deacon calls on the whole congregation to stand in fear of God to hear the Gospel, and the whole congregation responds to his call and glorifies God. Also, the priest takes off his shoes to read the Gospel, for he is standing in the presence of God. Then, after the reading, the whole congregation files past to kiss the Gospel, held open in the priest's hand, with joy and tears. In the early Church the people would do this out of their zeal, fear, and love of the Gospel, and it has remained as a ritual in the Church.

He who has tasted the power of the Gospel in his life does not consider this excessive, but does even more to show his veneration:

There are those who always fast to read the Gospel.

There are those who, when they read the Gospel alone, always kneel.

There are those who always read it with weeping and tears.

God's directions to us are most often given through the reading and hearing of the Gospel, when we are in a state of humility and when we pray with an open heart.

2.

Christ of the Old and New Testaments[1]

The overall course of history is subject to God

The Old Testament, from the first chapter of Genesis on, shows that human history is a movement of creation and development, beginning from God and then becoming established in man. God continues to direct and control it with great precision according to His particular design and will, so that the movement of history, whether in the life of an individual or a generation or a nation, is clearly seen to be in complete and perfect subjection to the will of God and His foreknowledge. "God is "The King of ages" (1 Tm. 1:17) and everything takes place "according to the definite plan and foreknowledge of God" (Ac. 2:23). God also irresistably determines the movement of time for man: "having determined allotted periods and the boundaries of their habitation" (Ac. 17:26).

Transcendence of history in God

The movement of time appears to be independent and so seems free and unrelated to man, for the sun rises and sets,

[1]Throughout Advent the Church turns its thoughts to the relationship between the Old and New Testaments and the confirmation of the prophecies related to the incarnation of the Word. The season of Advent begins in the Coptic Orthodox Church on Nov. 25.

39

whether man wills it or not, and the year goes by, summer
and winter change apart from his wishes. Time even appears
to disdain man as if it had authority over him. In fact, however, God has subjected to man the passage of time, with all
its imposing greatness, so that man might fashion from it his
spiritual history, as it stretches across the ages and rises at
last above the passage of time itself, for he will be united with
God in eternal life, where there will be neither sun nor monn,
summer nor winter (cf. Rv. 21:23). Christ pointed to this
culmination when He said, "Heaven and earth will pass away,
but my words will not pass away" (Mt. 24:35).

Time as a movement in material reality, with its heaven
and its earth, is dead and transient, but in the human reality it
is living, lasting history, the history of salvation, the history
of the Word of God that never returns void. It is a movement that begins from God and ends in God, taking with it
redeemed humankind: "Before I formed you in the womb I
knew you, and before you were born I consecrated you"
(Jr. 1:5).

So if man moves according to the will of God, that is,
in harmony with the knowledge of God and His consecration,
then he rises above the movement of time and actually subdues it to the will of God, transforming the hours and days
and years into a history of salvation, a divine age, everlasting
life in the Kingdom of God: "Behold, now is the acceptable
time; behold, now is the day of salvation" (2 Co. 6:2).

The man who challenges the will of God and deliberately
disregards His knowledge and His holiness falls beneath the
march of time and becomes a dead part of a dead age. And
the man who is forced to submit to the movement of time
serves the will of God, but under compulsion, neither perceiving nor willing it nor being gladdened by it. He is like the
chill of winter or the heat of summer, momentous but at the
same time insignificant, serving the growth of the creation but
unloved by it, giving it energy, strength, and renewal, while
he himself is dead.

God's intervention in human history

The whole of the Old Testament is a living history that clearly and brilliantly tells the story of God's constant condescension, and His communication with man to raise him above the passage of dead time. This He accomplished by intervening through His word, making of the succession of years and generations a sacred, living history, the history of God with man and of man with God.

This is to say that the whole Torah is both the history of the action of the word of God in humanity and a history of the acts of humans in accordance with God's word, or against it. In both of these ways God was clearly revealed with all His attributes. It is as if the passage of time in the Old Testament led eventually to the revelation of God with all His attributes to man and in man when the will of God was obeyed, but also when it was rejected; man's rejection of the will of God was a new factor through which God's ability to bring mankind into submission could be revealed.

Every person is part of every book of the Bible

When we read the books of the Bible, they appear outwardly to be purely a history of temporal events. But if we consider deeply their purpose and aim, and relate ourselves to what we read, we discover that they intend to reveal the living God Himself in our own selves. We see ourselves as we are, and then we begin to see God as He is, especially when He is compared with us. What is the value, then, of God's being revealed to man? In this lies the whole secret of the Torah and the Gospel, and the essence of the value of humankind and the whole of history. "And this is eternal life, that they know thee the only true God, and Jesus Christ whom thou hast sent" (Jn. 17:3).

Drawing near to God in time through knowledge

God is truth and life and everlasting light. The knowledge of truth is participation in truth; the knoweldge of life is life; the knowledge of light is illumination. Man, through his loss of the knowledge of God, has lost the truth within himself, and has lost eternal life and light. He can no longer perceive anything but the passage of time sweeping past him and over-powering him till he falls dead beneath it. All possible avenues to the knowledge of God were prepared for man; it is the knowledge of God that saves man from falling under the dominion of time and its illusory finality in death. The knowledge of God is His constant revelation in the minds and hearts of all people through communication and love, and it is also being in constant joyful union with the source of being that is a guarantee of life and immortality. This inevitably causes us to rise above the passage of time and death till we sense that we are greater than time, higher than events, and truer and more lasting than death.

The rational word and the Word incarnate

But in order for the revelation of God to be more perfect, all generations had to experience the knowledge of God through all the ages, so in the end all would know God as complete truth beyond the perception of the individual and know an eternal life broader than time and the life of one person. For this it was necessary that humankind pass through two ages, or testaments, of life with God, each quite distinct from the other.

The first, which we call the Old Testament, represents the stage of indirect revelation through the rational word. The second, which we call the New Testament, represents direct revelation through the Word incarnate.

The Epistle to the Hebrews summarizes the difference between the Old and New Testaments: "In many and various ways God spoke of old to our fathers by the prophets; but in these last days He has spoken to us by a Son" (Heb. 1:1,2). This makes it clear that revelation in the Old Testament was indirect revelation, that is, revelation to the prophets through the inspired word of God at different times ("of old") and through different events ("in many and various ways"). But the New Testament is God's direct self-revelation ("by a Son") beyond history ("He has spoken to us"). It cannot be outdated or restricted by history ("in these last days") because the Word became flesh. The revelation of God in the two testaments took place on two distinct and completely complementary levels: the first is the objective historical level, founded on the rational inspired word, through the passage of time, changing events, and successive generations; the second is the level of real self-revelation, founded on the incarnation of the timeless and eternal Word of God. This second is a direct revelation, beyond time, through the incarnation, with the appearance of God in the flesh, God Himself remaining unchanged.

*The revelation of God in man and in Himself
in the two testaments*

The historical method God used to reveal Himself in the Old Testament had three basic components:

The first was to give the people as a nation specific temporal promises regarding the nation's existence and its relations with other nations. God would fulfill the promises in the time specified through the instrumentality of judges, rulers, and kings, whose movements and actions God had planned so they would perceive Him through His perfect direction of affairs.

Second were the commandments, legislation, and religious and liturgical regulations, including the necessary consecration of ministers and the anointing of priests, to teach the people and draw them closer to God, so they would sense Him through purification.

The third was to give prophecies and spiritual direction concerning the future of the people in their ongoing relationship with God and their mission to the other peoples of the earth. This was accomplished through prophets who spoke by the Spirit of God, so that by repenting and drawing near to God they might know Him.

The amazing thing is that each of these three components appears in every book of the Bible, and deep study and meditation show that they constitute a clear and perfect plan with a logical method and a clear purpose.

The judges, rulers, and kings who succeeded each other in Israel over a period of two thousand years clearly had in common a divine authority, in spite of the moral and religious differences between them, and their many failures. Indeed, it is as if they were appointed by God to fulfill a single divine plan whether they individually succeeded or failed.

The same is true of the Levites and priests. In spite of their different ranks, functions, and qualities, and in spite of the failures of many, they were united by one duty, which they performed for the people and which God accepted regardless of whether they acted sincerely and willingly, or treacherously and rebelliously.

The same is true again of the words of the prophets. All the prophecies that were spoken, worthily or unworthily, throughout the Old Testament are testified to by Scripture as being the words of the Holy Spirit, and they were fulfilled in due time, even if the prophet was unclean and the people rejected the prophecy.

What is more, these three ways, exemplified in the king, the priest, and the prophet, which were the basis of the historical-pedagogical method God used to reveal Himself to the people of Israel through the ages, are bound together in a supreme unity of purpose that progresses with time. The kingdom in Israel, that is, the method of government and the way of life of the king, was what guaranteed the practice of the worship of God, the services of the sanctuary, the maintenance of the priesthood, the daily service of God and the fulfillment of all the priestly functions. This in turn was related to the utterances of the prophet regarding the soundness and correctness of the aims that motivated Israel as a people. The unity of Israel might therefore appear to be based on a system

—a system of monarchy, priesthood, and prophecy—but it was essentially a living organic unity. The king, the priest, and the prophet did not represent three systems, but were three members in a living body that God controlled and guided for a specific purpose and towards a goal vitally important to the whole world—the revelation of God Himself.

The divine plan that lay behind the establishment of this living body (a people led by a divinely anointed king, served by a divinely appointed priest, and inspired by a prophet who spoke by the Holy Spirit) may be summarized as God's desire to reveal Himself to the world through this living body that progressed through time and over many generations. God was revealed in the king through his kingship as a supreme governor and savior of the people. He was revealed in the priest through his priestly service as the conciliator and healer of the people. He was revealed in the prophet through his words and visions as the comforter and teacher of the people.

There is yet another amazing mystery for us to consider, which is also complementary to what has gone before. It is that God did not consider the people of Israel a body separate from Himself. He thought of them as His first-born son, for they were the first of the peoples of the world to be loved by God. He thought of them, too, as His beloved servant, for they were the first people to worship God according to a specific system of worship. He did not, however, see these things in the person of His kings or priests or prophets or even in the nation, which was itself rebellious. He saw them in the person of the Messiah, who was to fulfill the concept of kingship in the sense of just and divine rule, the concept of priesthood in the sense of redemption and salvation, and the concept of prophecy in the sense of a revelation of God that was direct and not dependent on allusions. He was to represent them as true sons before God by being the divine Son of God, while remaining at the same time according to the flesh a servant of God and a true Israelite by virtue of His being of the seed of Abraham, a son of David.

So the Messiah was reckoned from the beginning to be: (1) The everlasting King, in whose image David and all the divinely anointed kings were made, and in whom kingship would reach its culmination. The headship of the Kingdom of Israel was to rest upon His shoulders forever, in divine truth, not simply in history, for His throne would never pass away. "For to us a child is born, to us a son is given; and the government will be upon His shoulder, and His name will be called 'Wonderful Counselor, Mighty God, Everlasting Father, Prince of Peace.' Of the increase of His government and of peace there will be no end, upon the throne of David . . ." (Is. 9:6,7). (2) The Priest, in whose image every priest was made to serve before God as a mediator for the people, and in whom priesthood finds its culmination. Mediation settles upon His person, since He is the only mediator of redemption, forgiveness of sins, and eternal reconciliation between God and men. (3) The Prophet, in whose name every prophet prophesied and to whose coming in the fullness of time the prophets pointed. He was to be the culmination of all prophecy, all knowledge, and all the wisdom of this age, for Christ remains the living perfect revelation before God and man. There is therefore no more need of those who prophesy of Him, for all flesh has seen the salvation of God.

The New Testament points out the mysterious and perfect relationship between Israel as a people and the Messiah, that is Christ. All that was ascribed to Israel can be ascribed to the Messiah exactly and precisely. For example, God said of the Lord Jesus Christ when He returned from Egypt after taking refuge there with His mother and Joseph, "Out of Egypt have I called *my son*" (Mt. 2:15). This same word was said to the people of Israel when they left Egypt (cf. Ex. 4:22,23 ["Israel is *my first-born son* . . . let *my son go*"] and Ho. 11:1). It is as if the people of Israel were moving symbolically, acting out the work, life, and character of the coming Christ.

Indeed the characteristics held in common by the people of Israel and the Messiah extend into everything, even to the extent that prophecies addressed to Jacob, called Israel, were also to be understood as addressed to the Messiah. When the prophecy says "Jacob my servant" and "My servant Israel" (Is. 44:1; 49:3), it refers to the Messiah and can be explained and applied to both the Messiah and the people of Israel without any contradiction. This is the wondrous mystery that lies behind Christ's being called Son and Servant and at the same time King, Priest, and Prophet, for He is a true Israelite, or more precisely the true Israel, and He is indeed the Son of God.[2]

This shows the dynamic interrelation between the personality of the Messiah and the personality of the people of Israel. Every word spoken by God, every message, every action performed through His kings, His priests, and His prophets for the people of Israel was not at heart based on the person of the Messiah and but was intended to find its fulfillment and ultimate goal in Him, the everlasting King, the only Priest, and the Prophet who spoke His own words. On Him depended the whole existence and life of Israel.

Therefore the history of the people of Israel, with all the events that befell their kings, all the rites of their priests, and all the sayings of their prophets, is the history and knowledge of the Messiah Himself, but told symbolically in the form of a people chosen with care and love to represent God among the peoples of the earth and to proclaim His person and His mercy to the rest of the nations.

Even the tragedies of Israel, their captivity and constant disciplinary punishments throughout history, cannot be excluded from the sphere of positive action by which God was able to direct Israel slowly but surely forward drawing closer to the other peoples and kingdoms of the earth. This was in preparation for the unity with the other nations of the world which Israel had inevitably to undergo in the person of the Lord Jesus, the Messiah. When He perfected that union between Israel and the nations and reconciled the two in Himself on the cross, the historical mission of Israel came to an end. Or more precisely, the mission of the Messiah of history came to an end, and there began the Mission of the Christ of the nations, the Christ of eternal life.

So it is that the intrinsic and organic unity that exists

[2]"Who, though He was in the form of God, did not count equality with God a thing to be grasped, but emptied Himself, taking the form of a servant, being born in the likeness of men" (Ph. 2:6,7).

between the personality of Israel and the personality of Christ explains how all the historical events, all the legislation and rites, all the teachings and prophecies recorded by the Old Testament, although they are truly Israelite and particular to the people of Israel, cannot be explained or their purpose understood except in the person of Christ who is the origin and the end of Israel. As St. Paul the Apostle says, Christ is the end of the law given by Moses. He is correspondingly the end of the kingdom founded by David, and the end of the prophecies uttered by the prophets. Indeed He is the end of Israel itself and consequently the end of humankind, for "in Him all things hold together" (Col. 1:17).[3]

The Old Testament therefore prepares the way for Christ, portraying Him in time on the stage of history in the form of symbols. Historical events were at heart a prophecy pointing specifically to Christ until they were fulfilled in Him. Likewise all the priestly rites of worship continued to draw the human spirit closer to the mystery of Christ, the true Lamb, until they came to an abrupt end with the outpouring of His blood on the cross for all to see. The prophecies, too, constantly exposed the false material exterior that veiled the truth of the Kingdom of the coming Messiah, the Kingdom of grace and truth, spirit and life, until it finally appeared and we saw it and touched it with our hands in the Word of life, Jesus Christ, who is the Spirit of prophecy ("for the testimony of Jesus is the spirit of prophecy" [Rv. 19:10]).

Christ was and is the pivot around which the whole Torah, and indeed the whole of the history of human salvation, revolves. Perhaps among the finest images of the Messiah of Israel, the focus of the salvation and kingdom and glory of Israel, transformed into the image of the Messiah of the whole of humankind, covering the whole of the human creation, and becoming the focus of a salvation and glory and kingdom beyond the whole of this world, is Daniel's vision of the Messiah as the son of man: "I saw in the night visions, and behold, with the clouds of heaven there came one like a son of man, and He came to the Ancient of Days and was presented before him. And to Him was given dominion and

[3]And "in Him all the fullness of God was pleased to dwell" (Col. 1:19).

glory and kingdom, that all peoples, nations, and languages should serve Him; His dominion is an everlasting dominion which shall not be destroyed." (Dn. 7:13,14).

This truth was one of the most outstanding aspects of the teaching of the rabbis and inspired teachers of the Jews in the period before the birth of Christ. They insisted that there was no prophecy outside Christ. "All the prophets prophesied only concerning the days of the Messiah."[4] "The whole world was created for the Messiah."[5] And this same truth is the foundation of the New Testament, too. Christ Himself confirms it as a fact worthy of the utmost attention. "And beginning with Moses and all the prophets, He interpreted to them in all the Scriptures the things concerning Himself" (Lk. 24:27). This was the basis of the faith that was imprinted in the mind of the early Church. "All things were created through Him and for Him. He is before all things, and in Him all things hold together" (Col. 1:16,17).

When the Jewish teachers and rabbis realized this fact, they occupied themselves with gathering all the events and prophecies that pointed to the Messiah in the Scriptures, including things concerning the person of the Messiah Himself, His work, and His time in history. They collected 458 Messianic references, including 75 from the Pentateuch, 243 from the books of the prophets, and 138 from the histories of the patriarchs. These were recorded by the Sanhedrin. Regrettably, however, the later teachers and rabbis who lived immediately before the coming of Christ became absorbed in intricate expositions of these ambiguous texts concerning the Messiah and wandered off into fanciful deduction and nonsense that covered up the truth and obscured the features of the real person in whom the Messiah came. The prophecies pointing to the Messiah were distorted in the minds of the leaders; their perception of the truth was destroyed, their eyes were blinded to the vision of the light when it dawned. In addition, the spiritual awareness of the leaders faded because of their concentration on the outward forms of the law. The essence of religion among the priests, Pharisees, Sadducees,

[4]*The Rabbis of the Jewish Nation,* Sanh. 99-9.
[5]Ibid., Sanh. 98-6.

and scribes consisted in the precise keeping of the law, the repetition of the texts containing it, a strict adherence to the purification rites and other ritual observances, the recitation of short prayers, and a patriotic zeal for the recovery of their former glories, the kingdom, and their old supremacy. They could not consider any activity, action, or concern outside this sphere Messianic. Even the coming of the Messiah Himself, they thought, was simply to establish the ancient form of worship in precise detail and to fulfill their own hopes.

So Jewish worship departed from the true Messianic meaning it contained in the divine intention. The Scriptures and prophecies were no longer interpreted in their essential meaning; instead of concentrating on the person of the coming Messiah as the Savior of the world through Israel, they were understood to describe the Messiah who was to come as master of the world as the means of restoring the glory of the people of Israel.

So a conflict began between Christ and the Jewish leaders from the moment He appeared, in spite of His divine teaching Messiah as the Savior of the world through Israel, they avoided the subject of adherence to the petty details of the law, the purifications and superfluities of religion, and the worldly glory and supremacy of Israel, the farther He was moved from the priests, scholars, exegetes, and zealots among the people. They were fanatically devoted to their rites, their race, and their state, and it seemed to them that Christ did not have the qualities necessary for being the Messiah according to the way they imagined him, following their own inclination and corrupt purposes.

Nevertheless, this tarnishing of the essential meaning of faith in the Messiah among groups of priests, scribes, Pharisees, and Sadducees was not universal. There remained a part of the people of Israel, including leaders and other pious men, who still kept the pure spirit of worship and held on to the faithful promises of God. They longed in fervent faith for the coming of the Messiah as they perceived Him through their study of the prophets and the early inspired teachers. The New Testament, at the beginning of the

Gospels, gives us examples of these faithful ones: the old Simeon, Anna the prophetess, Zechariah the priest, Elizabeth, and the holy Virgin Mary.

3.

The Christ of History: A Living Christ

> But who do you say I am? . . . You are the Christ, the Son of the living God.
> (Mt. 16:15,16)

The birth of Christ, His death, and His resurrection were supernatural incidents that eclipsed their historical size, and it is here that their direct impact on all humanity has surpassed all measure of human logic. As for the character of Jesus, it suffices to consider what the disciples arrived at after the resurrection of Christ in the testimony they gave at their trial before the scribes and the elders of the Jews: "There is salvation in no one else, for there is no other name under heaven given among men by which we must be saved" (Ac. 4:12).

Therefore we should pay extreme attention when the Gospel relates to us the life of Jesus Christ. For what we read in the Gospels of St. Matthew and St. Luke of a human birth that occurred in the essence of history is again placed by St. John in a divine context that transcends history. For the birth of the child Jesus to Matthew and Luke is to John the incarnation of the Word that exists from the beginning.

Likewise in the case of His death, while the three synoptic Gospels relate the narrative of Christ's death from the viewpoint of the individual and human history of Jesus, the fourth Gospel steps out to elevate it above the level of individual history, and discloses in it the mystery of divine redemption that has encompassed the entire human race:

So the chief priests and the Pharisees gathered the
council. . . . But one of them, Caiaphas, who was
high priest that year, said to them, "You know nothing
at all; you do not understand that it is expedient for
you that one man should die for the people [in favor
of the Romans] and that the whole nation should not
perish" [that the Romans should usurp Israel]. He did
not say this of his own accord, but being high priest
that year he *prophesied that Jesus should die for the
nation* [in favor of God], and not for the nation
only, but to *gather into one* [Christ] *the children of
God who are scattered abroad* [all the peoples of the
world]. (Jn. 11:47-52)

We can thus perceive and feel in the very core of the
Gospels how history and eternity are merged together in such
amazing consistency. For history was, and still is, history. It
relates nothing but the past with its incidents, dead and
elapsed as they are, impressed on days, months ,and years. It
has always been impossible for people to conceive that history
and eternity would one day merge together, at which time
history would pose erect—in the person of Jesus Christ—
standing on its feet, alive and life-giving, efficacious, tower-
ing, interwoven with the very depths of God and eternity,
bearing the mortal past of man within an eternal and immortal life that fades not.

History—or time—was the point at which the story of
every creation is brought to a halt (being created, living, and
dying). This had been the case till—in the fullness of time—
a child named Jesus was born, recorded in history at an hour
of a day, a day of a month, a month of a year. He was
registered as a citizen in the records of the imperial census.
After two thousand years, ever since His birth and according
to the records of the Gospels, manifest incidents have begun
to show persistently and in conspicuous signs that here and
in this child a new history of humankind was ushered in!
A mystery that includes heaven and its unseen creatures, and
even extends throughout eternity and God!

This is how the Gospel of St. Luke records it for us:

And in that region there were shepherds out in the field, keeping watch over their flock by night. And an angel of the Lord appeared to them, and the glory of the Lord shone around them, and they were filled with fear. And the angel said to them, "Be not afraid; for behold, I bring you good news of a great joy which will come to all the people; for to you is born this day in the city of David a Savior, who is Christ the Lord. And this will be a sign for you: you will find a babe wrapped in swaddling cloths and lying in a manger." And suddenly there was with the angel a multitude of heavenly host praising God and saying, "Glory to God in the highest, and on earth peace among men with whom he is pleased!" (Lk. 2:8-14)

This heavenly event was the first outspoken violation of the confinement of humanity's field and of its ability to record history on the level of time. The angels' violation of the scope of man's vision and hearing is something that did not originally belong to history or to man's vision or hearing. It is clear that He who is born is of an existence that, once it took place on the human and mundane level in the manger of Bethlehem, immediately broke through the divine and heavenly existence. This then revealed its effect to the highest.

The angel here undertakes a task of extreme peculiarity, for he appears as an evangelist in the service of men, and thus undertakes—by virtue of orders issued by God—to remind everyone of the importance of *this day* in the history of humankind as a day of "great joy" from which all will continue to draw all their pleasure on earth. For the day of Christ's nativity is in its divine context the nativity of a Savior. The angel here enters for the first time into history as a recorder of days, yet in the meantime he discloses the value of such time hidden in the nature of the one who is born, not as a day of mankind but as a "day of salvation," a "great joy," a "pleasure among men." For with the birth of this Savior Child the days of sorrow are over, and those of happiness have begun. The age of man's disobedience is brought to an end, and that of the glorification of God is begun on earth by people as it is in heaven by the angels—even on the same footing! Yet, though a temporal starting point may appear in the angel's greeting "today," it is actually a commencement of a post-historic era, the history of eternal salvation, the history of the divine joy which will be poured out on earth and will never be taken away from the human heart.

Thus, the violation of man's world on the part of the angels and the multitude of heavenly hosts is in fact the beginning of man's entrance into the world of heaven, into the world of the angels and of God in the person of the one who was born to transcend the limits of time and place. In other words, the birth of Christ was the beginning of a reconciliation between two worlds, God with His angels on the one hand, and man with his sorrows on the other—the starting point of the revelation of that which is in heaven and the manifestation of the invisible.

It is from the Nativity that the evangelists started to write the history of Christ. But let no one think that the Gospel is a book of history that can be placed at the level of analysis and abstract verification. Historians and researchers who allow this illusion have stumbled at the verification of the person of Christ, who had already given a warning against approaching Him without faith, saying: "Blessed is he who takes no offense at me" (Lk. 7:23). For the eternity of Christ can by no means be recorded in the history of humankind without the elements of faith and inspiration that elevate history to the level of immortality.

The evangelists recorded God's history, not man's. They recorded the fulfillment of God's eternal promises of ages before, which were realized in their specified time in Jesus Christ His Son, who has been given to our earth by God in a flesh like ours. His advent had been predicted by all the prophets in the Holy Scriptures, which had been engraved by the Holy Spirit on the hearts of men and women of faith, preserving and guarding them strictly throughout successive ages till the day of His appearance.

The history of Christ is itself the history of God in respect to human salvation. Christ in Himself is the Word of God to man, as expressed in the Epistle to the Hebrews: "But in these last days He has spoken to us by a Son" (Heb. 1.2).

Though the life history of Christ the "Savior" might seem as though it were a history registered in time in the form of events that are confined within time and space, it is in fact the manifestation of God in the very essence of mankind, the manifestation of heaven on earth, of eternity in the fullness of time.

The Gospels appear to be a narrative written by four persons engaged in a thorough investigation of all that took place. Yet the Holy Spirit who inspired the evangelists while leaving them to portray Christ out of their own vision, experience, and observation, was in the meantime exerting control by Himself and through Himself in each and every view and experience, linking them with their divine source in a subtle allusion or an elucidation by means of which He revealed the mystery of the eternity through history, the mystery of the invisible in the visible, and even the mystery of the Deity in the flesh. Thus the Gospel never fails to reveal the outstanding personality of Christ. It is by no means difficult, even for the unlettered simple people, to perceive it by their spirits. Such personality transcends history; it stretches beyond the events and circumstances related in the Gospels. It is ever alive and effective, for it reveals itself as the personality of the Son of the living God in every line of the Gospel.

The Holy Spirit managed to transmit the experience of the evangelists and their observation through Himself as vividly as they accepted the experience and the observation with ineffable joy, entrusting them to the depths of faith. St. John the Apostle discloses to us the truthfulness of the feeling that flowed in him while writing the Gospel:

> That which was from the beginning, which we have heard, which we have seen with our eyes, which we have looked upon and touched with our hands, concerning the word of life—the life was made manifest, and we saw it, and testify to it, and proclaim to you the eternal life which was with the Father and was made manifest to us—that which we have seen and

heard we proclaim also to you, so that you may have
fellowship with us; and our fellowship is with the
Father and with His Son Jesus Christ. And we are
writing this that your joy may be complete. (1 Jn.
1:1-4)

Hence, the reader of the Gospel should hold fast to the
Spirit who inspired the text, and should by no means overlook
this factor while moving from history toward eternity, cross-
ing over with the visible to the invisible; otherwise he would
remain lost within the content of history, seeking the one who
is alive among the dead!

It is utterly impossible—according to the expository tradition of the Gospels—that anyone should conceive of Christ as
Lord except by the Holy Spirit. Likewise, Christ cannot reveal
Himself to anyone except through the heavenly Father. This
discloses to us the extent of the profound, substantial, and
infinite relationship of the Father, the Son, and the Holy
Spirit, not only in their personal entity, but also in relation
to the capability of their manifestation; it is only in His
totality that God may be revealed.

Hence, the incarnation of Christ, His birth, and His entry
into the essence of human history have rendered the Gospel
capable of moving between history and eternity with feasibility
and a mystery that is beyond reason. This, then, makes God
available to human knowledge after the isolation, exile,
separation, and even hostility in which all had lived far from
the only holy, absolute, and unknowable God.

Therefore, let it not be forgotten that the merging of
eternity and history in a realistic, tangible, and lively manner
was totally unprecedented. In the birth of Jesus, God has
been personally revealed. In it, as well, the invisible has been
seen and the unknowable has become known in a vivid manifestation of the glory of God.

Yet it is necessary for us always to draw attention to the
fact that anyone who enters into the Gospel on the level of a
mere historical investigation that searches, scrutinizes, and
analyzes Christ, is overlooking another major element in the
approach to the Gospel. The evangelists wrote the Gospels

and verified their history while fixing their gaze upon Christ as a Lord and God whom they beheld alive in their eyes and hearts. It is thus that the Gospel came out of their hands, not as a meticulous text of a precise history that related things concerning a man named Jesus, but—quite to the contrary— to relate the living reality that stood before their eyes and hearts (i.e., the reality of the Lord Jesus Christ, the Son of the living God who filled their being, emotions, and faith) which had been recorded in their memory in utmost fidelity and precision. In this way they were able to prove to believers that the living Jesus Christ who was raised from the dead in glory was God beyond all doubt, the selfsame Jesus who was born in Bethlehem, lived in Nazareth, preached in Galilee, and was crucified in Jerusalem.

It is therefore indispensable for the reader of the Gospels to place before his eyes this living reality before plunging into their message, that history might thus be transfigured before him. For the Gospels are—before being books of his- tory—books of faith. Hence the belief in the *person* of Jesus Christ unveils all the mysteries of the Gospel and solves all its historical problems as a narrative that was written two thousand years ago. We have thus perceived, and can perceive every day, that the Gospel is revealed in more profundity, grace, and insight to the simple-hearted of firm faith.

Yet the Gospel does not reveal the truth as a general hypothesis that may be accepted or rejected as a whole. Rather, it addresses every heart privately and personally, thus revealing the truth to every man according to his spiritual stature, the competence of his faith, and his acceptance of the truth, in a continuous flow of revelation that grows by faith and time.

It is thus fitting that the reader of the Gospel approach the truth recorded in it from its writer's perspective and spirit, receiving the words of the Spirit within them. It is not our intention, however, to make it hard for the reader; rather, this is the mystery of the Gospel that we are disclosing here. If the reader obeys the Spirit of the Gospel, commits himself to confirm it, and subdues his mind to the truth, then the truth will be transfigured before him exactly as the writer

beheld it. It is then that the reader will be touched by the
current of the Spirit in the Gospel and by its mystical tide,
which launches the reader's mind and heart from the *word*
directly to the *person* of Jesus Christ face to face.

Thus is the miracle of the Gospel fulfilled: "Then He
opened their minds to understand the Scriptures" (Lk.
24:45). Here history is transfigured and Christ is manifested
as a Deity by the demonstration of the Spirit within our
hearts.

Starting from this point (i.e. from alertness to the spirit
of the Gospel writer and a free submission to the Holy Spirit
who directs the words and gives them shape) we move on to
the indispensability of alertness to the words of Christ Himself which He uttered and stressed calmly and firmly, for by
mere alertness of the heart to these words we can feel the
personality of Christ Himself. Christ was actually *uttering
Himself* in every word and saying!

Whenever we become sensitive to His proclamation
of the relation that binds Him to God, we become conscious,
in a sure and firm sense, of the mystery of His eternal sonship
to God. Let us hear Him say: "My *Father* who is in heaven,"
"My heavenly *Father* will do," "I must be in my *Father's*
house," "My *Father* is working still, and I am working," "My
Father who has given them to me," "I have shown you many
good works from the *Father*," "I am the true vine, and my
Father is the vinedresser," "Abba, *Father*." We can here
sense—with no difficulty whatsoever—that the relationship
between Christ and God is eternal and superior to His human
state, and was undoubtedly existent prior to His birth in
Bethlehem.

The words of the Gospel writers are in themselves
magnanimous, but they indicate—with facility and simplicity
—that their speaker is of even greater magnanimity. The
theological import that these terms point to is profound and
serious. Yet it is by no means hard for the peruser or hearer
to feel that the mind that fashioned and uttered them is of
greater profundity and seriousness. The boldness of expression
here is beyond all comprehension, yet it is a confident and
meek boldness that leads logic to accept without effort that

Christ is but telling the truth, authoritatively expressing Himself with no affectation. Truly, the Christ speaking in the Gospel is speaking of Himself, the Truth, God! Christ *is* the Word of God!

This truth (the eternal sonship of Christ to God) Christ firmly established in the minds of His disciples so that all would perceive in it the mystery of His personal relationship to the Father, a mystery that would be in itself a medium drawing us closer *in Him* to God as a Father of ours as well.

Christ lays stress upon another fact of extreme importance, the manifestation of the Kingdom of God and the relation it bears to His advent in our world. The first sermon spoken by Christ to the world was: "Repent, for the Kingdom of Heaven [God] is at hand" (Mt. 4:17), thus referring to Himself. Throughout His life on earth He undertook to stress emphatically that the Kingdom of God had already begun, had already come, and was imminent. He proclaimed the inauguration of the age of God's Kingdom by His advent in the world, and indicated that His incarnation and birth was humanity's actual entry into the sphere of the Kingdom of God. Consequently, this means the entry of everyone who is united to Him in faith, a fact the angels emphasized on the day He was born: "Glory to God in the highest, and *on earth* peace among men with whom he is pleased!" (Lk. 2:14). Here the initiation of earth and man into the sphere of God's Kingdom and peace signifies the entry of the Kingdom of God into man's world.

Christ continually emphasized this till the day of His crucifixion when He stood before Pilate: "Pilate said to Him, 'So you are a king? Jesus answered, 'You say that I am a king. For this I was born, and for this I have come into the world . . .' " (Jn. 18:37).

It is only when we remember that He stood before Pilate that we apprehend the graveness and awesomeness of the accusation that Pilate would legally hold against Him to crucify Him for His claim: "I am a *King*."

Let us also not forget that He emphasized that He was a King while the cross was there before Him, the soldiers getting ready to crucify Him, and the cup of gall being mixed and prepared! How can we forget the back that was stripped bare, the whip, His head being struck and spit at? In front of all this there stood Christ, whom we still hear insisting, "I am a *King,* for this I have been *born* and for this I have come to the world!" And now let us shut our eyes for a moment and imagine this scene anew, and listen closely to hear Him pronounce the awesome declaration with His confident voice. It is now that a feeling of faith permeates us and permits us to understand that this is really the Son of God and that His Kingdom is an eternal one that will never dwindle and is not of this world. And if by His birth the Kingdom of God entered into our world, it is by His death that we entered the Kingdom of God in His heavens.

And now back again to where we started. We are once more in Bethlehem in a humble house rented by Joseph after the birth of Jesus. The Virgin is sitting with the child Jesus on her lap. He is nearly two years old. It is evening and darkness covers the house and the town. Suddenly there appears a light as bright as lightning that fills countryside and house. Joseph rushes quickly outside where he sees an extraordinarily bright star that has halted exactly above the house, as if it were pointing with its rays to the place where the child is. Joseph immediately perceives that it suggests a revelation. No sooner does he come in to tell the Virgin than he hears a stirring in the lane and at the door of the house. He then goes out to see a striking scene: a caravan of camels with all its trappings led by a band of slaves and carrying old men whose appearance betrays a sense of grandeur and wealth; they are princes from the orient. They dismount while their faces effuse joy and good cheer. They seem to be tired from their long journey. They then step forward to ask Joseph: Is there a child in the house nearly two years of age? whose annunciation came from heaven, whose mother is a virgin, and who the prophets spoke of? Joseph answers them with his finger at his mouth and takes them in haste into the house where the child and His mother are. To his amazement he finds the face of the child shining as if a ray of the star has penetrated the wall and is figured there upon His face; His mother he finds in an effusion of light, as if heaven were split open.

The Magi (the wise men) prostrate themselves at once and stand before the child singing a sweet melody, in reverence beyond all comprehension, while their faces radiate joy and their tears flow over their white beards as though they were shining with light.

They then approach the child, every prince with a gift in his hands. The first prostrates himself and opens his treasure: packed gold like that with which they adorn the crowns of kings. The second then prostrates himself and in his hands is a box of frankincense of a fragrant smell, which they sprinkle on the hands of the child who looks like a priest bearing a message. Then comes the third who prostrates himself and who in his hands bears a bundle of myrrh, like that presented to Him at the day of His crucifixion; it may even be that which they kept for Him for the day of His Passion!

I cannot help but wonder at those wise men and their gifts, and even more at the one who sent them and guided them!

Once again, the Spirit is there before us uttering, but with no tongue. For the gold in the hands of the Magi, as the narrative goes, is no more than money, wealth, greeting, or gift. But according to the Spirit it is an act of coronation and royalty with which the child was crowned while in the cradle, so Christ may be ever truthful. Did we not hear Him tell Pilate: "I am a *king,* and for this I was *born* and for this I have come to the world" (Jn. 18:37)?

I am awed also at the Gospel and its content; its end turns around to illuminate the beginning, and the latter in turn sheds its powerful, bright light to lead in facility to the end of the narrative. This is how the Spirit flows in between the lines and words and moves about among chapters. Blessed are those who follow the Spirit to walk in the light; it is to them that the mystery of Christ is unveiled.

4.

The Hidden Aspect of the Nativity

The coming Kingdom

The New Testament and Christianity do not stand in opposition to the Old Testament and Judaism. Rather, the New Testament is the declaration and fulfillment of all the promises and mysteries of the Old in the Messiah, the Kingdom of God, and salvation.

> For I tell you that Christ became a servant to the circumcised to show God's truthfulness, in order to confirm the promises given to the patriarchs, and in order that the Gentiles might glorify God for His mercy. As it is written, "Therefore I will praise Thee among the Gentiles, and sing to Thy name," and again it is said, "Rejoice, O Gentiles, with His people," and again, "Praise the Lord, all Gentiles, and let all the peoples praise Him"; and further Isaiah says, "The root of Jesse shall come, He who rises to rule the Gentiles; in Him shall the Gentiles hope." (Rm. 15:8-12)

In our time, the Church in the world among all nations is the revelation and fulfillment of the hopes of all the writings of the Old Testament concerning the Kingdom of God, where Christ the Head rules and governs the world-wide Kingdom of salvation. The whole hope of the people of Israel, with all their prophets and institutions, was focused on the salvation of the whole world. That salvation is now taking place through the Church.

It is also clear that throughout the Old Testament there is a development of the conception of the coming Kingdom of God and of the way the Messiah is understood and prophesied. This is why, when John the Baptist began to preach repentance and the Kingdom of God, the crowds gathered around him in numbers unprecedented in the ministries of all the other prophets. The conscious expectation of the Kingdom had reached maturity and was very strong. We see the same expectancy and acute sense of imminence in the declarations of Simeon and the prophetess Anna. The spirit of prophecy also spoke by the lips of Zechariah, Elizabeth, and John, confirming that the Kingdom was indeed at hand. But John the Baptist was completely honest with himself and his followers saying, "I am not the Messiah!"

We must not forget that Jesus at the beginning of His ministry was received unhesitatingly as the Messiah of salvation because of the truthfulness and faithfulness of John the Baptist; all those who were John's followers, even his closest disciples, went over to the Messiah.

All the people received Christ as the King who came in the Name of the Lord, the Son of David, to announce the beginning of the Kingdom of the Messiah, which they knew would last forever. When He hesitated to reveal Himself, they showed no hesitation in carrying Him off to make Him King by force. But He slipped away from them, because their understanding of salvation and the reign of God was incomplete and erroneous.

All this shows how far faith in the doctrine of the coming Kingdom of God had permeated the minds of the people, even the Gentiles. The common people always have an acute awareness that God is at work, as the saying goes: "The voice of God is heard in the voice of the people."

It is also clear that throughout the history of Israel there is a strong link between times of grief and exile and the painful chastisements of God on one hand and the blossoming of hope in the coming of the Messiah and in salvation

on the other. For those who long for salvation are those who
have tasted the bitterness of exile, whether in body, mind, or
spirit.

A quick glance at the Psalms, especially "The Lord reigns;
let the earth rejoice" (Ps. 97:1) and "The Lord reigns; let
the peoples tremble" (Ps. 99:1), will reveal how eagerly
they waited and how hard they tried to discern the coming
king through the darkness of history and events. And we
find this not only in the Psalms, but also in the prophecies,
which constantly point to the Kingdom of God and the coming Messiah who was to rule the whole earth in justice and
righteousness and gather the nations under the banner,
shepherding the redeemed into His fold where all would
praise and serve Him.

Whenever morality declined and conscience became corrupt, when the pillars of society, that is the leaders, collapsed
and circumstances deteriorated, then hopes rose that the
king would come to reform the moral life of the nations and
heal the sickness that had stricken the people with moral
decay. Prophecies would sometimes speak more clearly of
it being God Himself who would rule and strike the rebellious nations with the rod of His wrath, annihilating the
hypocrites with a mere breath from His mouth. And God
would become the everlasting Father of the redeemed who
would be forgiven and would be called the Prince of peace
on earth.

Then comes the Messiah and performs all the works that
had been written of. The Gospel records that John sent his
disciples to ask, "Are you the one who is to come or shall
we look for another?" In other words, "Are you the redeemer, the savior, the healer who will rule over Israel and
subdue all the nations and peoples?" Christ's reply was,
"Go and tell John what you hear and see: the blind receive
their sight and the lame walk, lepers are cleansed and the
deaf hear, and the dead are raised up, and the poor have
good news preached to them. And blessed is he who takes
no offense at me" (Mt. 11:4-6). That is, "Blessed is he
who receives Christ as the coming King of righteousness."
"We have found him of whom Moses in the law and also

the prophets wrote, Jesus of Nazareth, the son of Joseph
(Jn. 1:45). Thus the spiritual meaning of the Kingdom of
God in the New Testament is that it is a very precious inheritance we have received from the prophets, the dear hope
in which generations past died.

The Kingdom of God, which the coming Messiah was
about to reveal and proclaim, was the deepest and dearest
hope of all, not only for the prophets, but for all the rabbis
and teachers and for all the people. Questions were answered
and inquiries replied on the basis of the coming Kingdom:
"The [Samaritan] woman said, 'I know that Messiah is
coming (He who is called Christ); when He comes, He will
show us all things' " (Jn. 4:25).

The visible aspect of the Nativity

We have habitually concentrated our meditations about
the birth of Christ on what took place visibly in history, for
the Word became flesh and we beheld His glory. Life was
manifested and we saw it with our eyes and touched it with
our hands; God appeared in the flesh.

The shepherds received a sign from heaven and left to go
and see the wonder in the cave—a baby wrapped in swaddling
cloths and lying in a manger, declared to be the One who
would save His people from their sins. The Magi came too,
traveling a great distance, guided by a heavenly star that was
moved by the power from on high, so that the testimony to
the Savior of the world should come from outside Israel, at
a time when the leaders and rabbis failed to discern and
proclaim their Savior.

The hidden aspect of the Nativity of Christ

But now we shall consider what took place invisibly on
the day Christ was born. It has been overwhelmingly demonstrated on the stage of history and time, as well as in the
hearts of the Apostles, the saints, and the whole Church, that

He who was born was indeed the coming King, the Savior, the Redeemer, the Bearer of the key to the house of David, who when He closes no one can open, and when He opens no one can close. This is an everlasting Kingdom which will never pass away, according to the vision of the prophet Daniel (cf. Dn. 6:26).

This is the other aspect of the birth of Christ, for in Christ was fulfilled God's promise of the beginning of the age of salvation, and the manifestation on earth of the Kingdom of God, guided and governed by Him; this was the Kingdom spoken of tirelessly by the prophets. The hosts of heaven declared salvation: "There is born to you a Savior," and the Magi declared the everlasting Kingdom: "Where is He who has been born King of the Jews? ... We have come to worship Him" (Mt. 2:2).

So we can behold the hidden face of the day of the Nativity: Thrones were destroyed and others set up. One age ended and another began, as the Virgin Mary said in her immortal song of praise: "He has put down the mighty from their thrones, and exalted those of low degree." "He has shown strength with His arm" (Lk. 1:52,51). At the Annunciation the angel also declared clearly and gloriously, "He will be great, and will be called the Son of the Most High; and the Lord God will give to Him the throne of His father David, and He will reign over the house of Jacob forever; and of His Kingdom there will be no end" (Lk. 1:32,33).

How amazing that the saving Kingdom of Christ should be proclaimed while He was still in the womb, and confirmed in many ways, first by the angel, then by the Virgin at the beginning of her pregnancy, and then by Zechariah the priest, and by Elizabeth. On the day of His birth it was reconfirmed by the heavenly hosts and the Magi, who bore the hardships of their long journey so that they might see the King of the Jews and worship Him, and present gifts expressing the essence of their faith in His Kingdom.

Christ's constant emphasis on the reality of the Kingdom

The other aspect of the birth of the Christ child, swaddled and lying in a manger, is this Kingdom, proclaimed from heaven, and by angels and rulers, the Kingdom which Christ was born to establish and rule for man. Christ was born with the key to the house of David upon His shoulder, according to the angel's words to the Virgin, "And the Lord God will give to Him the throne of His father David, and He will reign over the house of Jacob forever; and of His Kingdom there will be no end" (Lk. 1:32,33).

We must focus our attention on this other aspect because it is the essence of the meaning of the Nativity. If we read carefully we find that it is this other aspect that dominates the Gospel and the whole of Scripture. Christ Himself in His sayings and parables concentrated on nothing else in the way He concentrated on the Kingdom of God. The Kingdom of God was even the subject with which His ministry began. "From that time Jesus began to preach, saying, "Repent, for the Kingdom of heaven is at hand" (Mt. 4:17). If we recall the events recorded in the Gospel we find that in Christ's final teachings, after the resurrection and during the forty days when He appeared to His disciples, He spoke with them of the Kingdom of God (Ac. 1:3). You remember, too, the parables of Christ concerning the Kingdom that are found throughout the Gospel, in which the Lord tried to explain and describe the inexplicable and indescribable Kingdom of God by using all kinds of illustrations. The Lord's concern to present these parables of the Kingdom shows the great significance of the concept of the Kingdom as Christ saw it. No single parable could describe the Kingdom of God; even all the parables together were insufficient. Otherwise Christ would not have needed to spend forty days, in the fullness of His resurrection and transfiguration, explaining again the things of the Kingdom of God after He had already taught about the Kingdom constantly for three and a half years, both explicitly and in parables.

The Kingdom of God, after all that has been said in the

Gospel and all the explanations, remains ever new and awaiting fulfillment. When all our words and all their meanings
come to an end, the fact of the Kingdom remains unchanged.
It is a life that cannot be described but needs to be lived.
This is why, however much we talk about the Kingdom, we
find that words fail us. The Kingdom remains something
needed by the soul much more than it is needed by the mind
or the imagination.

Christ and His parables of the Kingdom

When Christ was born of the Virgin He was in outward
appearance and ordinary man, though surrounded by extraordinary events. This was and still is the opinion of many,
for they see in Christ a great man born of a virgin in holiness by an incomprehensible miracle. The miracle is regarded
in the same way as any unfathomable riddle. Exactly the same
thing happened when Christ set forth His parables of the
Kingdom. Some saw them simply as parables containing
enigmatic wisdom, but Christ would then go to the inner
circle of His followers and explicitly reveal to them the
secret of the parables He told as riddles about the Kingdom
of God. "And when His disciples asked Him what this
parable meant, He said, 'To you it has been given to know
the secrets of the Kingdom of God; but for others they are
in parables, so that seeing they may not see, and hearing
they may not understand' " (Lk. 8:9,10).

So Christ in His birth, crucifixion, and resurrection was
like one of the parables He used to tell about the Kingdom
of God. The Christ born of the Virgin was outwardly no
more than a proverb of riddle, but those who have eyes to
see and ears to hear perceive the other aspect of the Nativity:
God appeared in the flesh, as the child who was born revealed the mystery of heaven, the mystery of the power, authority, and glory of God, and the stamp of His nature
(cf. Heb. 1:3).

Amazingly, God provides the sceptics with an example
to reproach them for their foolishness. The example, which

comes very early to bear witness to the inscrutable mystery
of Christ, is of the Magi who came from the distant east
to prostrate themselves before the child born King in
Bethlehem. The Magi were fully aware of the hidden aspect of the Nativity. Their eyes were opened to see His
star in the sky; their ears were opened to hear the mystery. So they understood everything, obeyed the vision,
and did not rebel against the call.

This is Christ born in Bethlehem. A mystery both visible
and hidden. You may content yourself with the outward
vision: a story, a maxim, a riddle. So it is if you go no further
than the Christ of history in any of the Gospel stories. But
if eyes and ears are opened, Christ and His birth assume
another intangible significance that no book or human mind
can contain, for He becomes like the mystery contained in His
parables of the Kingdom, a source of vision that is endlessly
satisfying, and a source of understanding and wisdom beyond
all reason. He is the grain of wheat, as He said of Himself
and as He said too in His parable of the Kingdom of God,
the grain that contains the mystery of death and resurrection
and the mystery of hunger and satiety.

All this is to say that Christ's preoccupation with explaining the Kingdom of God was because He was revealing Himself and explaining His birth. If we could go back to all the
parables of Christ and in the Spirit penetrate them deeply,
we would discover much of the mystery of Christ Himself.
When the Lord sent His disciples out to preach, He showed
in the way He commissioned them the extent of the relationship that exists between the Kingdom and Christ: "Go and
preach the Kingdom." "You are witnesses to me." Whoever
receives you receives me, and whoever receives me receives
Him who sent me." Here Christ makes Himself the focus
of the preaching of the Kingdom. It is true that the Kingdom
is "the Kingdom of my Father," but "I am the Way" and
"no one comes to the Father except by me." "He who has
not the Son has not the Father."

The Christ child reveals the mysteries of the Kingdom

It is true that the Kingdom of God is power, but the Christ born in Bethlehem reveals how light-giving, calm, and humble that power is.

It is true that the Kingdom of God is a system, an organization, a law, but the Christ born in Bethlehem reveals the love, sympathy, humility, and self-sacrifice of the heart that was given to explode the forces of that system, organization, and law.

It is true that the Kingdom of God is the logically supreme power and absolute divine authority, heavenly government, and divine decree, but what happened in Bethlehem reveals to us that the Kingdom of God, for all its awesomeness and heavenly supremacy, is no longer alien to our race or beyond our vision or hard to hear. The everlasting miracle has taken place, the wonder beyond all human logic has been fullfiilled and the heavens have announced the message: "To you is born this day in the city of David a Savior, who is Christ the Lord. And this will be a sign for you; you will find a babe wrapped in swaddling cloths and lying in a manger" (Lk. 2:11,12).

The newborn Christ in the manger reveals to us the other face of the Kingdom and how it is that in great simplicity and humility and in supreme divine kindness, salvation was to be worked out in that Kingdom.

The simplicity of the newborn Christ and the Kingdom

The manifestation of the Kingdom as a power and organization, a system and authority in the person of Christ, appearing in humility in His birth in Bethlehem, gives us an acute sense of the Kingdom. As Christ Himself emphatically said, "The Kingdom of Heaven has drawn near to you" (Mt. 4:17), "The Lord is at hand." Indeed, we should perceive that the child who is now before us in Bethlehem is utterly simple. He can be won over by love,

just as any child we may embrace and kiss. This is the way
God chose to represent the nearness and simplicity of the
Kingdom of Heaven. Or rather, it is in the supreme simplicity
that the Kingdom is brought near and the possibility is introduced of its being taken through the birth of Christ in
that very accessible stable, and not in the palaces of kings
behind walls and closed doors kept by servants and cham-
berlains.

Indeed, I believe that all those who have tasted the
heavenly gift and become partakers of the Holy Spirit, have
tasted the good word of God and the powers of the age to
come (cf. Heb. 6:4,5). They clearly perceive now the truth
of this saying and how freely the heavenly gift has been
granted and how easy it is to attain. As the Scripture says:
"The Kingdom of heaven has suffered violence, and men
of violence take it by force" (Mt. 11:12). For just as one
may embrace a newborn child, so may we acquire the Holy
Spirit in our hearts.

The Kingdom and Christ within our grasp

Let us look together close and long into the eyes of the
infant Jesus wrapped in swaddling bands and lying in the
manger, for in His eyes we will see the other side of the
Nativity. We will see the Kingdom in all its depth and
height. We look at Him and He looks at us with supreme
simplicity and acceptance. Carry the child Jesus in your
arms to perceive how light is the Kingdom even though
it be a yoke to be worn and a burden to be carried.

If you would really believe that the Kingdom of God is
personified in Jesus Christ, hear the words of the Lord
Himself linking the Kingdom with Himself. He spoke of
the devout who forsook everything "for my sake and the
sake of the Gospel" (Mk. 10:29), and it is clear of course
that the Gospel is the preaching of the Kingdom. The
disciples were very conscious of this reality linking the
Kingdom with Christ. St. Luke the evangelist wrote clearly,
"When they believed Philip as he preached good news about

the Kingdom of God and the name of Jesus Christ, they were baptized, both men and women" (Ac. 8:12).

The visible Kingdom and the unseen Kingdom

The Lord referred to this reality in its depth when He said to His disciples, "The Kingdom of God is in the midst of you" (Lk. 17:21), and when He said to St. Peter, "I will give you the keys of the Kingdom of Heaven" (Mt. 16:19). This was in reference to Peter's confession, "You are the Christ, the Son of the living God" (Mt. 16:16), for faith in Christ is the key to the Kingdom, according to the prophecies of "the key of the house of David" (Is. 22:22; Rv. 3:7).

But the truth of the unseen Kingdom was obscure to many, such as the simple women who used to serve Christ. The mother of the two sons of Zebedee, for example, seized a convenient opportunity to ask the Lord that her two sons sit on His right and left in the Kingdom!

This sense of the coming Kingdom, or the expectation that the Lord would suddenly be revealed in His Kingdom, was not alien to the atmosphere in which all the companions of Christ lived. The power of Christ was itself the manifestation of the Kingdom of God, and so the Kingdom repeatedly drew near to them after every miracle till it became an integral part of their consciousness. Eventually they said it must have been about to take place and became so fervent about it that they were in a state of acute expectancy and sometimes tension: "They supposed that the Kingdom of God was to appear immediately" (Lk. 19:11). So Christ began to teach them in parables that He still had a long way to go before He would return and that much time had to elapse before the Kingdom would be manifested. "A nobleman went into a far country to receive a kingdom and then return" (Lk. 19:12).

This sense of the imminence of salvation and the appearance of the Kingdom of God by the revelation of the visible Kingdom of Christ dominated all the disciples and the people at large during Christ's last days on earth, so that a week before the crucifixion the crowds cried out, "Hosanna! Blessed is He who comes in the name of the Lord! Blessed is the Kingdom of our father David that is coming! Hosanna in the highest!" (Mk. 11:9,10).

The Kingdom of God comes in power

But the shouts of the crowd came exactly fifty-seven days too soon for what took place on the day of Pentecost. The descent of the Holy Spirit in power from heaven was to bring about the Kingdom, though only in a partially visible way. Salvation took place from above, Christ was revealed as Savior and Redeemer, and the Kingdom of God became an inner reality filling the disciples and speaking through their lips in every language to every nation called to salvation. This bringing about of the Kingdom by the power of the Holy Spirit on the Day of Pentecost is what Christ referred to when He said, "There are some standing here who will not taste death before they see the Son of man coming in His Kingdom" (Mt. 16:28).

But we have already seen the angels announcing the appearance of this same Kingdom in another and deeper way at the moment of the birth of Christ in Bethlehem. They used the same words the children sing on Palm Sunday, when they cried with the hosts of heaven, "Glory to God in the highest, and on earth peace, goodwill towards men" and united the Kingdom of God in heaven with its appearance on earth. The angels' cry corresponds mysteriously with the chidren's chant: "Hosanna in the highest! Blessed is He who comes in the name of the Lord! Blessed is the Kingdom of our father David that is coming in the name of the Lord!"

The praise of the angels is a theological anthem

Here it is very important to perceive what the angels

meant by linking the glory of God in the highest with peace and goodwill on earth. Is this not the reality of the incarnation, the hidden mystery of the other aspect of the birth of Christ in the animals' stable? The binding together of heaven and earth, the invisible with the visible, and God with man, is the reality of the Nativity. It is the true manifestation of the Kingdom of God among humankind—Emmanuel, which means "God with us."

The hymn of the angels is not simply a song or joyful anthem. It is a theological declaration and a revelation of the true meaning of the mystery of Christ expressed angelically in a song of praise.

We find that in spite of the incarnation of the Word, the only Son of God, that is, His becoming man, or in the words of St. Paul the Apostle, "in Him the whole fullness of deity dwells bodily" (Col. 2:9) and "[God] was manifested in the flesh" (Tm. 3:16)—in spite of this, we perceive in the song of the angels that the union did not abolish Heaven and earth. Rather, glory continued being given to God on high, and at the same time and for the same reason the fullness of peace and goodwill came upon humankind. For the union that took place in the person of Christ does not abolish anything, but increases the glory given to God in Heaven because of His humility and condescension, just as our peace and gladness were increased by the love, redemption, and salvation that came to an earth full of hardship and grief. This is what the Kingdom and its manifestation mean, that we should acquire on earth the whole intention of God and His heavenly goodwill. This is the essence of the prayer the Lord taught His disciples, so that they would meditate on it whenever they prayed: "Thy Kingdom come, Thy will be done, on earth as it is in heaven."

Because Christ united in Himself the will of the Father with the will of humankind and made of them His own single will, He was able to grant us the great grace by which we become able to fulfill the will of God in our life on earth, and receive constantly in the depths of our hearts, through the mystery of the body and blood, and according to the extent to which we pray, the Kingdom of God that we are always praying will come.

If we go back to the praise of the angels, "Glory to God in the highest, and on earth peace, goodwill towards men," we can see in it a sure promise that the prayer "Our Father, which art in heaven ...," that we pray all the time will be answered, but answered in our Lord Jesus Christ. Just as the angels sang and proclaimed that because of the birth of Christ in Bethlehem glory is ascribed to God in the highest and peace granted on earth, and good will towards all, so at the mystery of the incarnation of Christ, we ask in confidence, "Thy Kingdom come, Thy will be done, on earth as it is in heaven."

It is Christ who is the secret of these two supreme bonds between Heaven and earth and between God and man.

Let us look upon the Christ child born in the stable. Let us consider how simple and humble was His entry into the world, for it is through this very simplicity and humility that we are able to break through to the other side of this wondrous birth and see God. We are able to grasp the mystery of the will of God, and the mystery of the Kingdom, which is now within our reach, like this meek child lying in the manger.

5.

The Righteousness of Humility[1]

"Let us now fulfill our righteousness"

We shall continue[1] from what we said at the Feast of the Nativity concerning our great need to always progress from faith expressed in words to faith expressed in experience. Remember how that evening we were able to see in the stature of the Christ child a new opportunity, even a new power, from which we could seek to acquire renewal, or rather healing, for the pride of our spirit, which has withered with age and whose wounds are festering. Remember how there opened before us on the Feast of the Nativity a door leading to a new life of fellowship with Christ in His infancy, to prepare us to enter into the Kingdom according to the condition laid down by the Lord: "If you do not become as little children you will not enter the Kingdom of Heaven."

Today, beloved, as we celebrate the baptism of the Lord in the Jordan, we see before us the fulfillment of the same experience that we entered into at the Nativity. Now Christ, as a young man of thirty, steps forward, with a childlike spirit that is quite amazing, to be baptized by a man, by John.

As a child, Christ had offered humankind an opening, or rather an effective source, from which one could draw power and inspiration to solve major problems: "Which is

[1]A sermon delivered in the church of Abba-Skheiron, in the Monastery of St. Macarius, in January 1976.

the greater?" It is a problem from which no one can escape; even the disciples themselves fell prey to it, and St.
Luke records for us the regrettable scene. "A dispute also
arose among them, which of them was to be regarded as
the greatest." And He said to them, "Rather let the greatest
among you become as the youngest, and the leader as one
who serves. For which is the greater, one who sits at table,
or one who serves? Is it not the one who sits at table? But
I am among you as one who serves" (Lk. 22:24-27).

Now, in His baptism, Christ offers us, as He bows His
head under the hand of John, a solution to a deeper and
more serious problem: "Which is the most righteous?" I
call this a deeper and more serious problem, because "Which
is the greatest?" is a problem related to outward ap-
pearances. It may happen that a man may avoid the problem by preferring his brother to himself before other people,
so that he should appear more humble or more righteous.
But the great disaster and danger lies in the problem "Which
is the most righteous?" Man, in his heart, always praises
himself, and it is hard for man to praise the righteousness
of another. But in the baptism of Christ we see this rule
strikingly reversed. Christ, the most righteous, presents Himself to John, who is totally lacking in righteousness (that
is divinity), and bowing His head in humility urges John
to consent to baptize Him.

Pay attention here, beloved, for when Christ says, "Let
it be so now; for thus it is fitting for us to fulfill all righteousness" (Mt. 3:15), He is not receiving righteousness from
John, but "fulfilling" all righteousness for John and the
whole human race. Here Christ, although He appears to
be receiving for Himself the anointing of baptism for
righteousness, is in fact, by His baptism, bringing about all
righteousness not for Himself but for any other person who
follows His example. Christ here, through His baptism,
adds righteousness to the account of humankind, the
righteousness of the submission of the greater to the lesser.
Christ here introduces to the human race a possibility that
did not exist before, the possibility of the submission of the
righteous to one who is less righteous. Through this sub-

mission a new righteousness was born, introduced by Christ to the world of human pride, and Christ counted it as "all righteousness."

Today Christ offers the greatest treatment for the greatest malady. By bowing His head under the hand of John, receiving from him the unction of baptism, He delivers to us the spirit of humility, or, as we may say more powerfully, the mystery of humility, which contains "the fulfillment of all righteousness."

In the eyes of God the people of Israel were basically characterized as a "thick-necked" and "stiff-necked" people. Stiff-necked toward whom? Toward God Himself. The people of Israel never bowed their heads under the hand of God, and they were not the last of the peoples of the earth to behave so. Christ came to heal the stiffness of the necks of the people of Israel and of all the world.

He bows His head simply, submissively, and quite willingly under the hand of John and delivers to us a divine balm with which to anoint our necks, so that we can be healed of the pain of pride and receive the mystery of "all righteousness." This is the secret balm, the divine and mysterious ointment, which, if we use it, restores to our necks the suppleness of childhood so that we always bow our heads in simplicity, seeking after all righteousness.

We notice, beloved, that Christ presented Himself to John as one needing to be baptized. This is clear when John says to Him, "I need to be baptized by You, and do You come to me?" (Mt. 3:14). That is, "You are coming to me like one in need." In fact Christ had no need to be baptized, nor any need for anything, including righteousness, but when He presented Himself for baptism as one in need, bowing His head in obedient submission, He revealed to us one of the mysteries of the fulfillment of righteousness. When we set out to perform an act of humility and submission, we must do so as one who is truly in need, not in condescension! Christ reveals and carries out not what is fitting for Him, but what is fitting for us and for our salvation and for the fulfillment of righteousness in our lives.

But I still feel, beloved, that I have not conveyed the full meaning of Christ's bowing His head to John.

This action of Christ's by the Jordan stirs our consciences deeply. I might almost say that by it Christ has this evening exposed our pride and revealed how far we are from understanding and practicing "true righteousness." How hard it is for a layworker or priest to bow his head to receive a blessing from the hand of one his equal! What Christ did went beyond all sense and logic. There was no fault in Him that He should bow His divine head under a human hand to be anointed.

By this submission, which supercedes all the logic of priesthood, Christ established a righteousness that excels every other righteousness in greatness, action, and warmth. He saw fit to record here in the Jordan, at the beginning of His public ministry, the firm foundation on which a successful ministry must be based, "the bowed head." This is borne out and confirmed by the parallel we find in what Christ did the night He instituted the mystery of the Lord's Supper, when He stooped down completely and sat on the ground to wash the disciples' feet. It is as if bowing the head in contrite submission is the formal beginning of every divine mystery, whether baptism or the eucharist.

The true significance of this point appears when we remember what Christ said to Peter when he tried to excuse himself from having his feet washed, thinking it was too much that he should stand like a master having Christ before him like a slave and servant. The Lord rebuked him: "If I do not wash you, you have no part in Me" (Jn. 13:8). The same thing happened at His baptism, when John tried to excuse himself from the task of laying hands on Christ's head and baptizing Him in the water. The Lord cut him short saying, "Let it be so now; for thus it is fitting for us to fulfill all righteousness" (Mt. 3:15). Christ's firm intention here to insist on the absolute necessity of His taking up a position before both John and Peter reveals to us the importance and seriousness of the mystery of humility and submission in serving the Church, in the priesthood and, in the Christian life in general. It is the basic way of

entering into righteousness. "For I have given you an ex-
ample, that you also should do as I have done to you...
If you know these things, blessed are you if you do them"
(Jn. 13:15,17).

The truth that we Christians must never forget is that
Christ here abruptly reveals the normal order of things to
make us vigilant. Christ here rejects the human concept
of justice and turns it upside down. He rejects every logic
of self-defense and pours scorn on it, for after He has bowed
His head beneath the hand of John we can no longer ask
with dignity, "Who is the greatest?" Our dignity lies in
our deliberate and insistant relinquishment of every dignity,
and in surrendering it to those who are less than we. We
can no longer uphold claims to leadership or priority or
privilege, for the exent to which we humble ourselves before the community is what establishes our righteousness
and our true leadership; our actions are to be commended
in proportion to the renunciation of our own worthiness.

John the Baptist's readiness to baptize Christ was an
act of obedience and submission that may be compared with
the humble and modest response of the Virgin Mary, when
God chose her to bear Christ. The obedience and submission
of John the Baptist to the Lord's command to baptize Him
prepared the way for Christ to enact, within the rite of the
mystery of baptism, the amazing mystery of humility, which
He called the mystery of the fulfillment of righteousness.
Here in the Jordan, as later when He washed the disciples'
feet, the Lord demonstrates His submission, like a slave,
under the hand of John to abolish the shame of man, who
refused to submit to the hand of God.

Once again we stop to contemplate how heaven was
moved by the humble acts of the Lord Jesus. When Christ
was born and laid in a manger in a stable, the heavens
opened, and the angel and the hosts of heaven appeared
to announce the good news of a great salvation and to
glorify God. Here at the Jordan the same thing happens.
The heavens open, the Holy Spirit appears visibly, and the
voice of the Father Himself announces the identity of
this Man bowing His head before John: "This is my be-

loved Son, with whom I am well pleased" (Mt. 3:17). So it is that, in so far as we on earth humble ourselves, God reveals Himself and with the angels of heaven gives us glory.

We notice too that the Holy Spirit, taking the form of a dove, alights on Christ as He bows Himself down. He does not appear as a tongue of flame as on the day of Pentecost, nor as a heavy hand upon the head as it happened to the Old Testament prophets, for the Holy Spirit chooses the form in which He appears according to the condition of the one He comes upon. The Spirit chose the form of the gentle dove to reveal the nature of the heart of Jesus and His great meekness, love, and humility.

How much we need today the meekness of this heart of Jesus as He stands bowing down before John in simple humility and submission, so that the Holy Spirit may come upon us in the form of a dove to bring us closer to the Jesus of the Jordan and unite our hearts together with that gentle, humble heart!

At the Nativity we took the meekness of infancy as a standard by which to live at all times as preparation for entering the Kingdom of Heaven. At the Jordan we take the bowed head of Christ as a standard by which we may be prepared to live in humble fellowship with the Holy Spirit, and as a vocation to fulfill in the world.

Just as Christ urges us to go back and remain always as children so that we can enter the Kingdom of Heaven, He urges us also to be as meek as doves. This is the anointing we need for service and for living in the world. Christ is always ready to give us the spirit of infant humility according to His stature in Bethlehem, and the spirit of the humility of the dove according to His stature in the Jordan, so that we can be prepared outwardly and inwardly to attain the full stature of Christ.

6.

Repentance and Asceticism in the Gospel[1]

Repentance is harmony with God

A man cannot return to God by his own ability alone: "No one can come to me unless the Father ... draws him" (Jn. 6:44). And in ancient times the prophet said, "Bring me back that I may be restored" (Jr. 31:18).

Nevertheless, God only draws those who are striving and longing for Him. Human will is a vital factor in repentance, because God, out of respect for human freedom, summons us without coercion or constraint: "Come to me all who labor" (Mt. 11:28), "Him who comes to Me I will not cast out" (Jn. 6:37), "If anyone thirst, let him come" (Jn. 7:37), "Return, faithless Israel ... Acknowledge your guilt ... Return, O faithless children" (Jr. 3:12-14).

Repentance is the coming together of the tranquil will of the God of love, which draws sinful man through the efficacy of the blood of Christ and the will of weary, fearful man who has a genuine desire to return to God.

This meeting between the will of God and the will of the sinner is a breakthrough. It enables human nature to receive earnestly the acts of divine mercy, love, and kindness, to feel them deeply and be greatly moved by an overwhelming mixture of feelings—thankfulness, helplessness, regret, love, amazement—so that in the end we can do nothing but surrender ourselves as captives to God forever.

[1]Published in *Great Lent,* April 1975.

Repentance can only end in union with God

The life of repentance is not simply a deliberate return to God. It is also the acceptance of an invitation to enter into a covenant of grace and the state of salvation. This entering is not limited by time and has no end, for the grace of God is beyond time and divine things can never be perfectly grasped. So it is that we constantly rediscover the new divine life and grow and continue to grow in it according to our own will and the will of God. It therefore follows that the life of repentance can only end in union with God.

So we must not understand repentance as being something only for a period of time, or as one of the phases of life. We should rather take it as a complete way of life, life with God.

Repentance is constant change

This becomes clearer when we realize that the word repentance is a rendering of the original Greek μετάνοια, which means literally a "change of thinking" or a "transformation of the spirit."

In practical terms, the Church understands it as a renewal of being, granted by God after baptism, through confession. That is to say, it is a process of constant upward progression in human nature, built on the individual's sense of sin and regret and confession of it. These are all means of self-abasement and humility, just as the act of repentance, which we call metania, is a total prostration with the face to the ground, whether it be directed to God or to man, as an expression of self-abasement and contrition.

So repentance conforms in practice to the Gospel: "whoever humbles himself will be exalted" (Mt. 23:12), for in so far as one continues in humility, he will continually progress on the upward way, and in this tension there is constant change. Repentance is a constant process of change in our being that abases us by our own will, but raises us up by grace. This is the vital meaning of the word metania. And so repentance is the opposite of self-righteousness. The latter produces a sense of self-sufficiency, so the process of inner change and upward progress is brought to a halt by the lack of a need for change. The "righteous" man considers that he is in a state of grace and has no sense of need for humility. This conforms with a contrasting saying of the Gospel, "whoever exalts himself will be humbled" (Mt. 23:12), since a change takes place in the reverse sense and one is in a state of constant spiritual decline.

Repentance as an actualization of baptism

The soul that does not practice inner change through a repentance built on contrition before God cannot enter into grace or perceive it. This is a sign of our hardness of heart, and is a harbinger of death. That is why repentance is of vital importance, drawing the line between life and death, like baptism itself. Indeed, some of the Fathers consider repentance to be more vital than baptism. We read in St. John Climacus:[2] "The spring of tears after baptism becomes, may we dare to say, greater than baptism itself." But St. John Climacus does not exaggerate, for repentance is the fruit of the grace of baptism from which it draws its mysterious power. That is to say, those who are without repentance are also without baptism, since repentance either establishes baptism or annuls it. This shows how vitally important repentance is.

Repentance is a work of grace

It must be pointed out quickly that the expression "the spring of tears," which St. John Climacus uses constantly to refer to repentance, and all that the Fathers say concerning weeping over one's sins refer to a work of grace and not to

[2]In the book *The Heavenly Ladder*, the seventh stage.

the striving of the individual. It is a gift, not a discipline. St. Isaac the Syrian calls it "the gift of tears" and it is a sign of fruitful repentance. Tears are a mystical indication of true joy, as the Lord showed when He said, "Blessed are you that weep now, for you shall laugh."

Tears that spring from hope are part of the mystery of repentance; they are evidence that the penitent has entered into grace and a secret sign that the state of true joy has been attained.

From this we can understand how tears can wash away sins, not because they are a work of the human will, since the greatest human work cannot atone for even the smallest sin, but because they are a gift of the Holy Spirit and a pure work of grace and reveal that the power of God has begun to penetrate deeply into our being. Tears are a clear sign of the process of inner change and also evidence of the truth and power of the mystery of repentance.

But let no one think that tears of repentance will be given without consecrating the mind and the will and longing constantly that the heart be turned to God. This is related to human freedom, for our determination to leave the life of sin and consecrate our life to God in love opens the door for many gifts to be given to us, including the gift of tears. St. John Climacus urges that the life of a repentant man, or monk, should be constantly aflame. "The wise and sincere monk is the one who does not allow his inner fire to be extinguished, and who right up to the day he leaves [this life] constantly kindles flame upon flame, ardor upon ardor, longing upon longing, and zeal upon zeal."

The Christian understanding of asceticism

The divine incarnation in itself may be taken as the highest expression of ascetic action, for it required the greatest possible degree of humility. The Son of God carried this out in Himself by deliberately relinquishing all the glory of His divinity and taking the form of a humble slave, a rejected servant.

Moreover, as a direct result of this, as the human will was totally united with the divine will, Christ completely conformed the human mind to the mind of God. This in itself may also be considered an act of asceticism, in the sense that it was an act of obedience by which Christ demonstrated definitively and practically His Sonship to God.

Asceticism is that constant working toward conforming the human will and mind to the will and mind of God. This definition is a guide for the ascetic life itself, for it indicates that every ascetic act that does not conform to the will of God is dogmatically erroneous, in view of the fact that the ultimate aim of the Christian life is union with God. This union begins from the first moment in the life with God, through obedience to the commandments in an attempt to submit human will to God and attain a submission that slowly conforms one to the mind of God.

7.

Repentance

*Repentance is but a second victory of
faith, and is itself a new testimony*

If humanity has enjoyed the early eras of faith and has
been revived by martyrdom as a seal of faith, there still
waits for it an age of repentance that will be one of its
most flourishing spiritual ages and will by no means be
less enjoyable or less flourishing than the early eras if
that repentance is practiced correctly.

Repentance is but a second victory of faith and is itself
a new testimony. Returning to the faith formerly held is
almost a greater joy than embracing it for the first time.
Look at the widow's joy after finding the lost penny (Lk.
15:8-10); look at the shepherd whose joy over finding his
one lost sheep was greater than the knowledge that he had
ninety-nine more in the sheepfold (Lk. 15:4-7). The Lord
teaches us that the return of a penitent to the bosom of Christ
is equal in its power and honor to the pleasure of having
a whole sheepfold (a whole Church).

God desired to endow repentance with double the honor,
happiness, pleasure, and joy so a sinner would not be des-
pondent or bashful at coming to the bosom of Christ, so
that the glory of the cross would prevail over the ignominy
of sin, and so that the meek God who is ready to justify
the ungodly would be glorified. Although a repenting sinner could hardly be noticed by the world, the Bible says
that the whole heaven welcomes a sinner's repentance and

rejoices at a person's justification. It is as if repentance is
the greatest of works humanity can take pride in, for a
penitent is that individual who has responded to God's
power of forgiveness and justification and has thus gained
through anguish the fruit of the cross and the sanctification
of God. Look how the penitent through contrition can give
joy to all of heaven and to the heart of God!

When saints perceived the honor pertaining to repentance and remorse—an honor originally belonging to sinners,
adulterers, and the slothful—they snatched it for their own,
and subdued themselves craftily and shrewdly to the severe
disciplines of repentance, as though they themselves were
slothful, so people would think repentance was the work
of saints, and contrition that of the righteous!

As for our wretched selves, we think that it is our
righteousness that introduces us to God, and that our virtue,
piety, learning, service, and zeal qualify us for communion
with the heavenly. We do not realize that "all [things] are
open and laid bare to the eyes of Him with whom we have to
do" (Heb. 4:13), that we have nothing good to approach God
with: "None is righteous, no, not one" (Rm. 3:10), and
that "all our righteous deeds are like a polluted garment"
(Is. 64:6).

If only we had known that Christ came to "justify the
ungodly (Rm. 4:5) and to call "her [beloved] who was
not beloved" (Rm. 9:25); if we could be sure of this, we
would immediately renounce all our righteousness, all our
false piety, all artificial ostentation, and would pose at
once as ungodly, not deeming our sin to be too great to be
washed away by His blood, nor our uncleanliness to be too
great a burden for His love.

It is no business of ours to justify the ungodly, for we
cannot. This is a divine action, a supernatural ability in-
comprhensible to us. It is the richness of heaven that has
been poured out with the blood of Christ into our hearts.
It is the richness of offering and total bountifulness. It is
the kindness of God mixed with overwhelming compassion
and love so much that it has been overcome by its own
affection, so much that it could not have mercy on its own

self, but would slay itself on the cross for the misery of sinners.

Justifying the ungodly is a divine mystery, one of the profoundest mysteries of salvation. It would be sufficient for us to believe only that God is able to justify the ungodly; this faith of ours would be considered righteousness on its own, let alone if we approached God as ungodly persons believing that we are to be justified by means of God's ability to justify and sanctify, which, if done, would bring us at once to the depth of the incomprehensible mystery of salvation.

Jesus Christ came to the world to save sinners!

The sinner—yes, the sinner who is but a quantity of filth mixed with lusts, evil, vanity, and the painful experience of wantonness. The sinner who is loathsome both to people and to himself is himself the cause of Christ's coming to the world.

The sinner who feels within himself a total deprivation of all that is holy, pure, and solemn because of sin, the sinner who is in his own eyes is in utter darkness, severed from the hope of salvation, from the light of life, and from the communion of saints, is himself the friend whom Jesus invited to dinner, the one who was asked to come out from behind the hedges, the one asked to be a partner in His wedding and an heir to God. God has promised not to remember any of his sins but to drop them into oblivion as a summer cloud that is swallowed up by the glare of the sun.

Is it not for him that He has crucified Himself and has borne misery and dereliction?

The wonderful power of Christ as a God who redeems and loves even to death can by no means be conceived or experienced exececpt in the person of the sinner who is cast on the ground and repudiated by all people!

Without the sinner we are able neither to comprehend the love of Christ, nor to measure its depth, nor can it show itself in an action which reveals the superlative quality of the divine love. Divine love appears as most dignified in our sight when we come to know it in its condescension to us while we are fallen into a state of misery.

For the sake of the sinner the mysteries of God's love have been unveiled and the richness of Christ has been opened to us, that richness which is offered for nothing, neither for gold nor for silver. How great is the poverty of the sinner, for it is solely the extreme destitution of the sinner that draws out the richness of Christ with a confidence similar to that of a hungry child when it draws milk out of its mother's breast!

Christ never enriches the one who is rich, nor does He feed the one who is satisfied, or justify the one who is righteous, or redeem the one who relies on his own power, or teach a scholar!

His richness is only for the poor and needy, to those who are cast away, the contemptible and in their own eyes wretched; His rich food is for the hungry, His righteousness for sinners, His right arm for the fallen, His knowledge for children and those belittled in their own eyes!

Whosoever is poor, hungry, sinful, fallen, or ignorant is the guest of Christ.

Christ has descended from the glory of His Kingdom to ask for those in the deepest depths, those who have reached the state of utter misery, perdition, and abominable darkness, those who have lost hope in themselves. In them is manifested His power of action and the power of His Godhead, when His slaughtered love steps out to bring the sinner out of the quagmire and the dunghill and when it steps out to sprinkle and wash with the holy blood every member that has been defiled. In such people is the righteousness of God glorified. In them He finds a field for compassion, mercy, and tenderness, and it is in the souls of those who are despised and cast off that His humility finds comfort, for in condescending to them He finds a work for His meekness.

If sinners only knew that they were the work of God and the pleasure of His heart: "We are His workmanship" (Eph. 2:10). If the sinner were sure that his rank in God's eyes was foremost among the cares of the Almighty and his dispensation from eternity, and that the mind of God had been preoccupied throughout the ages with his returning, and that the entire heaven waited in expectation for his return, he would never be ashamed of himself, condemn his ability, or procrastinate about his return.

If only the sinner knew that all his trespasses, transgressions and infirmities were but the point of God's compassion, pardon, and forgiveness, and that however great and atrocious they might be, they could never repel God's heart, extinguish His mercy, or fetter His love even for a single moment. If only the sinner knew this, he would never cling to his sin or seek isolation from God as a veil to cover his shame from seeing the face of Christ, who is trying to show love toward him and who is calling them!

Sin is no longer able to sever the sinner from God!

> Come now, and let us reason together, says the Lord: though your sins are like scarlet, they shall be as white as snow: though they are red like crimson, they shall become like wool.
>
> (Is. 1:18)

Such is God, always condescending to us, knowing how sin enfeebles the heart of the sinner and drives the sinner into a state of hiding and deadly shamefulness, in order that by repelling him from coming to God he might not live, he started calling the sinner importunately, and inviting him to confer and reason together.

The sinner thinks that sin prevents him from seeking God, but it is just for this that Christ has descended to ask for man! Is it not that God has come to the flesh of man to cure its illness and redeem him from the sin that has ruled over him and to raise him from the curse of death? Sin is no longer able to sever the sinner from God after He has sent His Son and paid the price—the whole price—on the cross. For it is the dismay of the sinner, his shame and false delusion, that hide the pierced side of Christ, in which the whole world may be purified several times!

Sin no longer has the right to exist or abide in our new nature; it is now like a stain on a garment, removed immediately in less than a wink of an eye when the sinner repents and seeks the face of God.

The sinner should not look around to seek any autonomous power or any medium other than the blood of Christ for entering into God to find redemption and forgiveness, lest he should insult the love of God and His superb mercy, or dishonor His omnipotence, His kindness, or His compassion. Even so, in all the saints of the Church and its penitents he can find assistance. For we have seen and heard and borne witness that the greatness of God's pardoning, His total forgiveness, and His ability to sanctify the sinner do not reach their utmost power and greatness except when the penitent reaches his utmost feebleness.

There exists a false sinner who speaks of himself as the great sinner and tells about his countless sins, yet within himself he does not perceive them as a reality, nor do they cause him any anguish or a pricking of conscience.

For such a person there exists no repentance even though he might have a thousand works and a thousand prayers every day, for Christ is a shrewd doctor who discerns the true patient from the one who pretends to be one.

Christ did not come only with water to wash away the dirt of the body, but also with water and blood to wash first of all the bleeding wounds of sin which have rent the heart and conscience of all humanity, then supply it with pure doses of His exhilirating blood, so that it might recover from its deadly faint, and rise and live.

When Isaiah the Prophet described our sins as crimson in color, he was actually referring to the bleeding of sin which has tinged the life of man with the color of death! For bleeding always puts a man in a state of despair and apprehension as someone stabbed in the heart or as a murderer whose hands have been smeared with blood; possessors of such sins, with bleeding, burdened, grieved, and desperate consciences are those invited by Isaiah to the depth of God's forgiveness and mercy. For these has Christ descended from the Father, to call them on the hill of

Calvary. Look at Him raising His arms on the cross to reveal the width of His bosom asking for those who are lost and banishing despondency from the hearts of the desperate.

Christ came to ask for real sinners sinking under the puncture of remorse and despair, giving no heed to liers who claimed to be penitent and condemned themselves before other people to gain more prestige by their humility so their fame would be glorified as penitents, though they were not.

It is to offer freedom to captives that Christ came, pursuing them to the hidden places of darkness, but if you have not yet felt the captivity of sin or if you are not aware of its darkness or have not been awakened by its smothering horror, how then can you cry out of the depths? If you do not cry in alarm, how then is the Savior to hear your voice and how is He to know your place?

Christ came to give sight to the blind. If you have not discovered the blindness of your heart and have not felt deprived of the divine light, but have tried to open the eyes of others while you yourself were blind, how is He to endow you with sight and where is He to give you the light?

The essence of repentance is an awareness of sin, a cry of the pain of crime, a certitude of the absence of light.

Repentance is but a fall into the hands of God!

I can will what is right, but I cannot do it.
(Rm. 7:18)

This is a terrible obstacle that has hindered a lot of people from stepping into repentance. At the gate of repentance stands the sinner gathering his will but finding no stock even to begin doing any good work; he then compares himself to those who have gained mercy and forgiveness, loses courage, and sinks into deep despondency and grief, seeing repentance as though it were a tedious task.

This is a device of the enemy; who said that repentance is a gathering of will, an act of courage, or power and activity? Is not repentance only a fall into the hands of God and at His feet in a fainting of will, with a wounded heart bleeding in regret, members being shattered by sin having no power to rise except by God's mercy?

The penitent is described by Christ as a stranger who has fallen into the hands of robbers in a foreign country. They strip him of his clothes, rob him, humiliate him, wound him, and leave him more dead than alive. The penitent is like a man stripped of the garment of his honor by the devil, whose will has therefore been stripped naked and whose members have been defiled. The devil robs him of his treasure—the treasure being the sanity of the mind, the light of insight, and the action of conscience—his person being humiliated, his fall disclosed, and his will shattered. Last of all, he wounds him deeply with lust to draw off his life quickly. At the end he leaves him a dead corpse unable to live! It is thus that the good Samaritan finds no occasion to ask questions or time to reproach, but immediately gathers him in his arms.

The good Samaritan in the parable (Lk. 10:30-37) is Christ, and our interpretation hits the mark exactly, for He does not upbraid him or ask him to perform any action, but comes to him personally where he fell and stoops over him with His affection, washes and dresses his wound by His own wound, stops his bleeding by His own bleeding, and pours upon him the oil of His compassion and of His life, carrying him on the arms of His mercy, offering him a ride to the inn of His Church, asking His angels to serve him, and expending His grace on him till he recovers.

Such is the penitent, a wretched man that has fallen on the way after being attacked by the oppression of man and the spite of the devil, and no longer able to do anything. After his strength has been drawn off, he finds room at the house of the Benign, room in His heart, room between His arms, on His beasts of burden, and in His Kingdom.

Christ has snatched sin from the entrails of man!

> Children have come to the birth, and there is no strength to bring them forth.
>
> (Is. 37:3)

Such also is the state of the sinner when he stands at the gate of repentance, agonizing in the hope of salvation and renewal of life. Yet, when he looks back at the past he has defiled he weeps, and when he aspires to the future he desires he faints, for he finds that feebleness has pervaded his entire being, and that he is no longer able to pull himself out of the mire, encompassed as he is by weakness. It is as if sin were the illness of withering that infects a plant, not leaving it till the gloom of death surrounds it from every side. This is exactly the nature of sin, which is cast into the entire being of a man to expel the spirit of life.

We are not only weakened by sin, but are already killed by it. And when Christ came He knew that we were "dead through the trespasses and sins" (Eph. 2:1). The person dead by sin was conceived in iniquity, and after a period of time the travail of death befell him. The birth of sin is a condemnation and true death felt by the sinner within himself. Christ has snatched sin from the bowels of sinners and has thus redeemed us from an inevitable death. In place of sin He has entered into the depths of our being and has been formed in our inmost parts. Our creation has been renewed; after death ruled over us, life now reigns in us and the travail of death is turned into the joy of life and deliverance. Christ underwent death to save us from such a death, and He is still carrying on His saving work.

Truly, it is unbelievable that a good man should die in place of a sinner, but God is not like man. All that is incredible and impossible God does when He "shows His love for us in that while we were yet sinners Christ died for us" (Rm. 5:8).

Therefore, the sin of the sinner, his extreme shame due

to that sin which is latent in his inmost being, the odor
of death suffusing his being because of the iniquity of his
former life, has all been measured by God in His deep love
and has found a solution for it in the coming down of His
Son to the flesh of the Virgin to bring fruit out of her womb,
a fruit of life instead of the fruit of sin that man had conceived. Instead of the feebleness of the travail of death
that Isaiah spoke of as though a man could not avoid it,
God overshadowed the Virgin womb with His Almighty
power so that it gave birth to a man. But what a birth, for
he is born God!

The sinner is asked to have confidence in the work of
Christ accomplished by His birth and His cross on account
of a person's sin, extreme feebleness, and death. Nothing is
asked of the sinner but to stretch out his hand like the
woman with an issue of blood (Lk. 8:43) and touch the
garment of the Savior. Then He will realize how the power
of the Lord comes forth to abide in him. Bleeding stops,
weakness is turned into strength, and death flees away
from before life!

Will you not stretch forth your hand to have your
share of power in order to cease being weak or dead? Remember this when you cry out with the chorus during Holy
Week: "The Lord is my strength and my song, and he has
become my salvation" (Ex. 15:2; Ps. 118:14).

If you want to know how the power of God might flow
in you, remember Jericho, how its walls collapsed not by
the sword or by war, but by the outcry of victory in the
name of the Lord. Remember also how the Red Sea was
split apart under the feet of the priests. The same power
of the Lord is always there for the weak, the distressed,
the perplexed, and oppressed.

Have you not known? Have you not heard? The
Lord is the everlasting God, the Creator of the ends
of the earth. He does not faint or grows weary, His
understanding is unsearchable.

He gives power to the faint, and to him who has
no might he increases strength.

Even youths shall faint and be weary, and young men shall fall exhausted; they who wait for the Lord shall renew their strength, they shall mount up with wings like eagles, they shall run and not be weary, they shall walk and not faint. (Is. 40:28-31)

There is no alternative to the aid coming down from above

For Thou didst cast me into the deep, into the heart of the seas, and the flood was round about me; all Thy waves and Thy billows passed over me. Then I said, "I am cast out from Thy presence. . . .
The waters closed in over me, the deep was round about me; weeds were wrapped about my head. . . .
I went down to the land whose bars closed upon me forever. . . .
When my soul fainted within me, I remembered the Lord; and my prayer came in unto thee. . . .
(Jon. 2:3-7)

This is the state of those who are torn apart by thoughts of remorse for their sins, yet who are suspicious of God's mercy, cast down like a drowned body driven away by a river of desperate conceptions and imaginations. Whenever they try to float to breathe the breath of life, heavy billows of mental darkness oppress them and cast them far away from their hope.

Their soul, as it were, is thus drowned more and more in endless worries; it is as if despair began to press upon them like a surrounding chaos, where sad pessimistic thoughts swoop down from all sides. Doubt, distress, and grief are wrapped around their minds as seaweed is wrapped around the neck of the drowned, blocking the means of deliverance so that there can be no salvation.

It is a bitter war for the sinner, who sinks under the cares of his many sins. When he thinks of salvation, the demons of darkness rise up to avenge themselves. No acumen avails the sinner, neither does the reasoning mind, or reading books, or consulting wise men. For the war is a mental one, and the mind is in an affliction of captivity; there is no alternative to the aid that comes down from above, from beyond reason, from there, from God who abides in the highest: "When my soul fainted within me, I remembered the Lord" (Jon. 2:7).

For those penitents in tribulation we present the verse of deliverance that will be for them an anchor in which they may trust, pulling the soul out of the abyss of perdition and leading it into the world of light, hope, and peace in the comfortable bosom of repentance: "Every sin and blasphemy will be forgiven men" (Mt. 12:31). Blessed is the living God who has previously known and measured every tribulation we are to undergo and all war devised against us; He has stooped with His ear always toward the voice of those crying to receive the first hint of appeal for help: "My prayer came to Thee, into Thy holy temple" (Jon. 2:7). Who is a God like ours so close to our prayer, so close to our supplication? "God is our refuge and strength, a very present help in trouble" (Ps. 46:1).

Confidence in Christ should be as perfect as Christ!

> I called to the Lord out of my distress, and He answered me; out of the belly of Sheol I cried, and Thou didst hear my voice.
> Then I said, "I am cast out of Thy presence; how shall I again look upon Thy Holy temple?"
> ... Yet Thou didst bring up my life from the Pit, O Lord my God. But I with the voice of thanksgiving will sacrifice to Thee; what I have vowed I will pay. Deliverance belongs to the Lord!
> (Jon. 2:2,4,6,9)

When the enemy molests us as those who have perished because of our blasphemies, we recall the saying of the Lord that He came to ask for and save that which had already perished. Whenever He says that we have lost hope for salvation because of the abiding of sin in our minds and our bodies, we recall that Christ died for sinners: "The blood of Jesus Christ His Son cleanses us from all sin" (1 Jn. 1:17). When He rebukes us by saying that we have been utterly polluted and have become wanton sinners, ungodly, and old hands at evil, we cling to the promise: "While we were still weak, at the right time Christ died for the ungodly" (Rm. 5:6).

Satan's logic is always a reversed logic; if the rationality of despair adopted by Satan implies that because of our being ungodly sinners we are destroyed, the reasoning of Christ is that because we are destroyed by every sin and every ungodliness we are saved by the blood of Christ!

It is from there that the repentant sinner's confidence in Christ springs with a rationality that remains unvanquished and unshaken. Yet such confidence in the ability of Christ to save us from the most dire states of despondency should be total and pure confidence in His person without reasoning or debating with the devil, regardless of the weakness of the will and of the flesh, and with no account of the loss or the price. The confidence in Christ should be as perfect as Christ, as vigorous as Christ, and as confident as Christ.

If Christ came to save us, then He must save us. It is impossible that He might not save us, for our salvation is the work of Christ, and it is impossible that Christ should abide within us and not work within us. The creed of our faith demands and is comprised of the belief that we are saved and have become penitents of Christ, for we maintain that Christ came to save sinners. And since we confess that we are chief among sinners, it is inevitable that we are to be the firstfruits of redeemed penitents. When we thus repent before Him every day, we repent not as the mighty and righteous, but as the ungodly and weak.

He came to ask for that which is already destroyed, and here we are, the destroyed, demanding Him and as dead clinging to His life.

He came to put Himself in the service of the weak

> I have become like a broken vessel . . . terror on every side. (Ps. 31:12,13)
> I loathe my life; I would not live forever. (Jb. 7:16)

Sin dissolves the will, spoils the personality, and loosens the bonds of the soul; we are no longer able to stand against the tyranny of lust and the allurement of sin.

For as the small mouse falls into the claws of the cat as soon as his eye catches him, so does the power of the sinner dissolve before the least gesture of lust. And as the heart of the antelope stops at seeing the lion and drops dead between his feet, so does the sinner give himself up to evil thoughts.

Whenever he decides to resist he falls, whenever he promises not to return he returns, no longer having confidence in himself. His power to do good becomes that on which he himself looks with disdain as on a broken vessel.

His hope in God dwindles away, and all his abilities in that respect dissolve and become like chaff blown away by the wind, like one without hope in the world.

It is thus that the enemy sometimes takes hold of the soul and binds it with fear, fear of that same sin, and drives it in what manner he wishes, from one sin to another. The soul, unable to raise any objection, follows him with a bereaved will, a fallen honor, hurt feelings, and a troubled conscience, with neither power to rise nor pleasure in falling.

Ah! What a poor soul! Don't you recall the glory of your first creation and that of your Maker? In His own image He formed you in courage, truth, sanctity, and righteousness.

But does God really know what befalls the sinner in such pain and distress? For an answer to this question let us hear Him say: "The spirit indeed is willing, but the flesh is weak" (Mt. 26:41). "Woman, has no one condemned you?...Neither do I condemn you; go, and do not sin again (Jn. 8:10,11). "Do you want to be healed?" (Jn. 5:6).

It is thus that our weakness and misery were known to Him from eternity, and He has come Himself and put Himself in the service of the weak and defeated sinners. He has kept His Holy Spirit in guard of their soul, working day and night to expel terror and fear from the hearts of sinners and turn their hearts into a temple and a place of His habitation.

The personality that has been broken asunder by sin is gathered again by the Spirit. The soul that had been humiliated by the devil, who had sneered at its authority and dissolved its will, is then touched by the grace of Christ, and hence is risen, renewed, and strengthened.

A single glance of Christ made Peter overcome his weakness and defeat before the servants and concubines, pull himself together and regain his will, which had been shattered as a broken vessel, so that his soul melted before threat. From the eyes of Christ he drew forth the power of repentance, from which he regained his wholeness.

Christ is still roaming among sinners healing every weakness and every infirmity of the soul. The Holy Spirit is ever ready to endow the tremulous with power from the highest. Grace is present every day to support trembling hands and feeble knees. And the love of Christ, when kindled in the repentant heart, changes it from a cowardly one to that of a martyr. How often has repentance turned feebleness, defeat, and surrender into testimony, witnessing and proclaiming the truth of the Gospel. The remembrance of previous horrors of the soul, of its despair and defeat are turned into a testimony of Christ's mercy. Terror as the motive force of sin and lust evaporates in smoke, and servile submission to the call of the company of evil is turned into advice and proclamation.

In this way the sinner puts off the image of corruption and is dressed in the new image by the hand of Christ, and the feeble, the cowardly, the timid, the defeated, and the

one who has no control over himself listen to the promise
from the mouth of the Omnipotent:

> Behold, I make you this day a fortified city, an
> iron pillar, and bronze walls...No man shall be
> able to stand before you all the days of your life...
> I will not fail you or forsake you. Be strong and of
> a good courage. (Jr. 1:18; Jos. 1:5,6)

*The power of repentance is in peristent strife to
acquire the spirit of life in Jesus Christ!*

> But I see in my members another law at war with
> the law of my mind, and making me captive to the
> law of sin which dwells in my members. Wretched
> man that I am! (Rm. 7:23,24)
> The dog turns back to his own vomit, and the
> sow is washed only to wallow in the mire. (2 Pet.
> 2:22)
> When shall I awake? I will seek another drink.
> (Prv. 23:35)

Much anxiety and care befall the soul when it discovers
the persistence, stubbornness, arrogance, and impertinence of
sin, and a resonance of sorrow mingled with oppressing despair
flow into the soul when it discovers, after recurring trials,
the futility of oaths, promises, works of penance, remorse,
and many tears.

But there is no avail; there stands the law of sanctity impressed by the hand of God on the heart of every person,
calling the depths of the soul incessantly: that there is no
comfort or rest whatever except in chastity, and no joy or
peace except in ceasing from sin! Any perversion away from
this law creates immediately great contention with the conscience, opposition to life itself, disagreement with the Spirit,
estrangement from the aim of creation, loss in the darkness
of thought, lack of balance in judgment of the nature of
things, mutiny against truth, and thus antagonism with the
Author of the law.

Nevertheless, it happens that man rashly starts—in foolish enthusiasm—by clashing with sin directly. But Oh, what sorrow when he discovers how crippled he is, and how tyrannical sin is! While he goes mad with enthusiasm he repeats the trial and is then greatly shocked to find out that the phantom of Satan is there embodied behind sin and latent in those organs that have become his own, ruling over the faculties of the soul and the motion of the flesh in a profound and organized manner, all of which having been planned a long time ago so that it acquired roots and law! Lastly—yes, at the very last—after man has exhausted all his efforts and displayed all his wiles and thought, he is then convinced that it is easier for him to contain water in a handkerchief, gather the wind in his palm, or go up into the sky with his feet than it is to control the law of sin by his own will, or to exert his rule over the powers of evil that are moving within the depths of his members!

It is here that Christ's action takes place, Christ alone has condemned sin in the flesh! "For the law of the Spirit of life in Christ Jesus has set me free from the law of sin and death" (Rm. 8:2).

Yet, it is in the persistent strife to acquire the Spirit of life in Christ Jesus that the power of repentance lies, where the flesh is to be emancipated from the law of sin by means of grace. Since we own the grace we can strive unto blood against sin, being sure that by grace we will be more than victors: "For I know whom I have believed" (2 Tm. 1:12).

It is not the aim of repentance that we be justified before God by means of remorse and outward repression of sin through acts of penance and of torturing the flesh, but that we be santified inwardly by the Spirit of Christ "that the sinful body might be destroyed" (Rm. 6:6) and freed from sin itself within the depths of conscience, that is power might vanish and fear of it might disappear, and that grace might be a guide to the movements of conscience, curbing the actions of the flesh, controlling the birth of thoughts, guiding asceticism, mingling itself with austerity, and sweetening regret.

It is not merely the forgiveness of sin that is the whole

action of grace within man, nor is it the ultimate aim of faith in Christ; but to withhold sin from the organs, that its power might cease to exist and its law might vanish from our nature, is the aim of repentance and of faith, and that pertains to the great sovereignty of grace.

"You know that He [Christ] appeared to take away sins" (1 Jn. 3:5).

On the cross Christ was wounded in His side to bring forth water and blood to all who believe and come to Him—water for washing away the impurity of sin, and blood to withhold its power.

How blessed is that day on which Christ's side was opened on the cross for the sinner to find in it his righteousness, his sanctity, and his redemption.

8.

The Deep Meaning of Fasting

Fasting and the imitation of Christ[1]

The Church imitates Christ. All that Christ has done the Church also does; He becomes its life. Christ's call to Matthew ("Follow me") was intended by Him to mean "Take my life for you." The Church has adopted this call as a scheme of its own.

Fasting, in the life and works of Christ, ranks as the first response to the act of unction and of being filled with the Holy Spirit. It represents the first battle in which Christ did away with His adversary, the prince of this world. In His forty days' experience of absolute fasting, Christ laid down for us the basis of our dealings with our enemy—along with all his allurements and vain illusions. "This kind cannot be driven out by anything but prayer and fasting" (Mk. 9:29). For when a person enters into prayerful fasting, Satan departs from the flesh.

As the Son of God, Christ did not need fasting, nor did He need an open confrontation with Satan or baptism or filling with the Holy Spirit. Yet He fulfilled everything for our sake so His life and deeds would become ours. If we know that Christ was baptized to "be revealed to Israel" (Jn. 1:31), it follows that being filled with the Holy Spirit meant "being tempted by the devil." This was so He could be

---

[1] "Fasting and the Imitation of Christ" originally appeared in Arabic in the *St. Mark Review*, March 1977, and was translated into English in the Monastery of St. Macarius (Feb. 1981). "Sanctify a Fast," the second part of this chapter, was published in 1965.

revealed before the spirits of darkness, and openly enter into combat with the devil on behalf of our race. Fasting was to elevate the flesh to the level of war with the spirits of evil, those powers that hold sway over our weaker part, the flesh.

The reader may notice that baptism, being filled with the Holy Spirit, and fasting form a fundamental and inseparable series of acts in Christ's life that culminated in perfect victory over Satan in preparation for his total annihilation by the cross.

It is then extremely important to accept and to feel the power of each of these three acts in our depths and draw from Christ their action in us as they worked in Him, so that His same life may identify with ours. The ultimate aim of baptism, of being filled with the Holy Spirit, and of fasting is that Christ Himself may dwell in us: "It is no longer I who live, but Christ lives in me" (Ga. 2:20).

In baptism the connection with our old Adam is cut off for us to receive our sonship to God in Christ. In being filled with the Holy Spirit, our connection with the devil and with the life of sin is cut off for us to receive the Spirit of life in Christ. And in fasting, the connection between instinct and Satan is cut off to give the flesh victory in its life according to the Spirit, in Christ.

We can never sever these three acts from each other; baptism grants spiritual fullness, and spiritual fullness grants (by fasting) victory for the flesh to walk in the Spirit. By the three together we live in Christ, and Christ lives in us.

The dimension of time in these three acts does not weaken their merging together, nor does it separate one from the other. Baptism in childhood, the spirit's fullness in mental and psychic maturity, and fasting, which concludes these three acts, could not be seen separately in the spiritual vision. Although they occur separately in time, out of human necessity, they are one act spiritually. They spring forth to us from Christ who is "One Act," "One Word." In all three acts, Christ dwells in us personally to give us His fullness, image, and life, so that we might *live Him* as One Act and One Word, and no longer live our own selves in our torn and disrupted image.

The point to understand is that fasting is a divine act of

life, which we receive from Christ complementary to baptism and fullness. Since its beginning the Church has been occupied with infusing into its own body the acts of Christ's life so they would become life-giving acts to all its members. If the Church imitates Christ in its life discipline, it is because it has been given grace and authority by God to possess Christ Himself as a life of its own. The Church, which is one with Christ, is a lively and efficacious image of the life of Christ. The Gospel describes it as the "bride of Christ" united with her Bridegroom. Though the Gospel declares that the Church has become one with Christ, it still reiterates that Christ will remain a Bridegroom on His own, no matter how much He offers Himself. Neither does Christ become a Church, nor the Church become a Christ. This confirms to us that we, as members of the body of Christ, always need to strive to acquire Christ to become more like Him and to be a bride "without spot," a betrothed "pure bride" in a perpetual state of betrothal like the Virgin who conceived and bore the Logos. Virginity here is "to keep onself unstained from the world" (Jm. 1:27). Being stained is the ungodly union between Satan and "the lust of the flesh," "the lust of the eyes," and the "pride of life" (1 Jn. 2:16). These three bonds were united and shattered by Christ during His fast on the Mount of Temptation. He gave us the shattered bonds as an inheritance to live out and carry into effect by fasting in the fullness of the Holy Spirit and in the sacrament of baptism.

Fasting in this sense is one of the fundamental phases that Christ underwent. We have never been able to claim that we live in the full maturity of Christ, or that Christ abides in us in His full measure, particularly if we overlook fasting. If baptism is one phase and crucifixion another, fasting is an extremely important stage between baptism and crucifixion. Fullness with the Holy Spirit, which Christ consummated by baptism, elevated the flesh to the level of extraordinary fasting, i.e. total deprivation of food and drink, utter seclusion and prayer. He thus raised the flesh to the stage of the cross.

It is impossible for us to carry our cross well and get through the temptation of the devil, the ordeal of the world, and the oppression of evil without fasting on the Mount of

Temptation. If being filled with the Holy Spirit does not qualify us for fasting we inevitably will be unable to bear the tribulation of the cross.

Here the Church's imitation of Christ's work is a necessary course of life for us, in which we may discover our salvation, strength, security, and victory. It was not for Himself that Christ was baptized, nor was it for Himself that He was crucified, and, consequently, it was not for Himself that He fasted forty days. The works of Christ—themselves a mighty and omnipotent power—have become sources of our salvation and life. Their power, however, is not imparted to us unless we experience and practice it. Those who are baptized put on Christ, those who are filled with the Holy Spirit live by means of Christ's life, and those who fast win Christ's victory over the prince of this world.

These liberating deeds of Christ and the extent to which they and His life influence us were most clearly declared by Christ Himself: "So if the Son makes you free, you will be free indeed" (Jn. 8:36). But how can the Son set us free from the world, the devil, and our ego except by dwelling in us and offering us His life, His works, and His victory? He reiterates often, "Abide in Me, and I in you." This in fact is the mutual action. We perform His deeds and live according to His example, and thereupon He imparts to us the power of His deeds, His life, and His example. Time and again He calls our attention: "Learn from me." Here He reveals that He has placed Himself as a model of life and works, as our "Forerunner," as the "firstfruits," that in everything we would be "like Him." He became like us so we would become like Him.

After fulfilling the course of our salvation with all these works, Christ stands there, face pale and wounds in His hands, feet, and side, and asks, "Do you believe in Me? Do you believe in the works I have done? Do you really accept Me as a Bridegroom?" He does not wait to hear us say "Yes" (only as a slothful bride); He invites us to a total communion with Him in suffering and glory alike. We thus have to prove our communion with Him in faith by having communion with Him in His works; only works testify to the genuineness of our faith. Yet He, as a true Bridegroom, did not leave us to invent works for ourselves but laid down the course of our works and life: "I am the way;" "He who *follows* me will not walk in darkness." Following Him is not so much an intellectual theory as it is tracking Him, imitating His works, and sharing communion in love and suffering.

We should notice that all the commandments of Christ regarding works—whether they be voluntary poverty, asceticism, renunciation of kindred, divestment, or bearing the cross —revolve around the person of Christ and end up in Him: "for My sake;" "come, follow Me!" "for My name's sake;" "be My disciple;" "come after Me;" "watch with Me."

Every work of Christ's, which He loved to do, He shares with us, or rather we share with Him on account of our love, our sacrifice, and our asceticism. It is from Him that all our works are derived: our asceticism from His asceticism, our fasting from His fasting, our love from His love. Ultimately, communion here is a realistic one which we develop daily by further imitating Him in mind and action and by deepening our awareness of Him in our life, making Him active within us while keeping us free, spontaneous, and quick in response —as a bride is to a bridegroom.

All the works we perform in the name of Christ, for His sake, and in imitation of Him—whether they be fasting, vigil, patience, endurance of suffering or persecution, service, sacrificial love, or crucifixion—are but a voluntary translation of the desire to imitate and unite with Christ ("Follow me"). They express communion in spirit, heart, and intention.

Here such works may be a way to express the overt offering of the entire soul to Christ in self-surrendering love and absolute discipleship, as it was for John, James his brother, and the rest of the disciples. They offered their lives and surrendered their souls to Christ the moment they saw and heard Him. They forsook their homes and jobs and became followers: "Lo, we have left our homes and followed You" (Lk. 18:28), becoming true partners of Christ's works, career, and suffering: "You are those who have continued with Me in My trials" (Lk. 22:28).

It is possible that such works as fasting, vigil, prayer,

service, or sacrifice may express a hidden love that is added
to life's daily tasks, such as earning one's living or bringing
up children. This is seen in the many who followed Christ
without official publicity, like Nicodemus, Joseph of Arima-
thea, Martha, Mary, Lazarus, and others whose high level of
love for Christ was by no means inferior to that of the
Apostles themselves. Yet, those who actually forsook everything and followed Christ are those who, by spiritual works,
most sublimely expressed a deep evaluation of Christ's person:
"We have left everything and followed you." The word
"followed" here denotes a shift from worldly work to
spiritual work; Christ is great enough to fill our entire life
and meet all our needs, becoming our sole work, our sole
hope, and our sole interest.

This is itself the same orthodox doctrine that the Church
received from the Apostles and addresses the zeal, fervor, and
agony of works, the main measure of every person's evaluation of Christ. The degree of concern and sincerity in spiritual
action is that which reveals the light emanating from Christ.
This consequently bears witness to the Father: "Let your light
so shine before men, that they may see your good works and
give glory to your Father who is in heaven" (Mt. 5:16).

The Apostles inherited the entire life of Christ, and were
eyewitnesses and partakers of His works and acts. They inherited the lengthy fasts they saw Christ Himself perform, as
Christ told them: "This kind cannot be driven out by anything but prayer and fasting" (Mk. 9:29). They inherited
night-long prayers ("Watch and pray"). They inherited agony
in prayer, with frequent prostrations and sweat like drops of
blood: "And being in an agony He prayed more earnestly;
and His sweat became like great drops of blood falling down
upon the ground . . . And He said to His disciples, 'Why
do you sleep? Rise and pray' " (Lk. 22:44-46). They inherited
endurance and patience amid the insults of the hierarchy
and the betrayal of comrades: "If they persecuted me they
will persecute you" (Jn. 15:20). They inherited ministry in
markets among the sick, the sinners, and the poor. They
inherited agony, suffering, and crucifixion, the most precious
and exquisite gift they inherited from Christ: "The cup that

I drink you will drink" (Mk. 10:39) ; "Then Paul answered, 'What are you doing, weeping and breaking my heart? For I am ready not only to be imprisoned but even to die at Jerusalem for the name of the Lord Jesus' " (Ac. 21:13). All these works they inherited not as acts apart from Christ, but as part and parcel of Him. Christ dwelt in their hearts through faith when they received the Holy Spirit, and they thus performed all the works of Christ according to His promises, even miracles and death.

The Church has inherited this living apostolic experience; it has inherited *Christ working in the Apostles.* So the importance, or rather the inevitability, of works in the Orthodox Church means that the Church focuses on Christ Himself working in us just as He did in the Apostles, doing the same deeds He did for our salvation. The Church believes in exactly what St. Paul meant when he said: "For God is at work in you, both to will and to work" (Ph. 2:13). It is equally confident that this also leads to St. Paul's words, "Do all to the glory of God" (1 Co. 10:31). It is through Christ and in His presence that works should be done; it is only the work of Christ that leads to the glory of God: "Jesus Christ is Lord, to the glory of God the Father" (Ph. 2:11).

It is now clear that the Orthodox Church's belief in works is nothing but faith in the perfect life in Christ. To this perfection belongs Christ's whole action and, better yet, even His entire mission and compassion for all humanity. Works, then, are not limited acts done by the human will to relieve the ego. The importance of works in Church thought is based on the fact that all works must spring from the will of Christ and be perfected by His power: "I can do all things in Him who strengthens me" (Ph. 4:13). Works must end up in the glory of God the Father. In other words, they must reveal Him and testify to Him: "That they may see your good works and give glory to your Father who is in heaven" (Mt. 5:16).

Henceforth, the concept of "faith and works" in the Orthodox Church is inseparable from the living person of Christ, who is the source of faith and works alike in human life. The utlimate end of both faith and works is the glorification of God the Father—an essential work that belongs exclusively to Christ: "Jesus Christ is Lord, to the glory of God the Father" (Ph. 2:11).

The law that correctly ensures that works are done through Christ and for the glory of the Father is the perfect imitation of Christ in every word, deed, and behavior. We should invoke the Spirit of Christ in everything by prayer, so works may be cleared of all impurities of self-will and human thought, and that they may be pure of flattery, hypocrisy, falsification, prejudice, and self-love, all of which cause works to be ineffectual, fruitless, and dead.

Sanctify a fast

When we strive to walk along the narrow way, we should be always conscious of being overshadowed by the cross, so that we can persevere, however great our hardship. To attain perseverence, it is essential that the sacrifices we offer never cease to be offered in love.

You should know that striving along the narrow way entails the risk of falling into either the negative sin of despair, or at the opposite extreme a sense of heroism and perfection in virtue. We can only reach genuine love by avoiding these two dangers that threaten our progress on the narrow way. This can be achieved if we discover how to overcome our own selves. Let us not feel sorry for our own selves lest we fall into despair, or praise ourselves lest we fall into the kind of heroism that the saints call vainglory.

If we delve deep into the essence of divine love, which is the model of love we intend to follow, we find that it only can be attained by self-denial to the point of self-renunciation, or even destruction.[2] This we learn from Christ on the cross and from His earlier life. To go on in love we must practice self-hatred[3] till we are no longer concerned with ourselves

[2]Destruction of the self is achieved by the elimination of its will. The degree to which we accept death is a measure of the extent self-will has been eliminated.

[3]Self-hatred is an inward attempt to deliver the personality from the captivity of the self, so that we can be united with the other (whether God or man) through love.

or any of the things of this world we used to count as gain.

Fasting is a test in which the personality defies the self. It is an exercise in which the self has to be forsaken and resisted by the whole being. Fasting may therefore be considered an act of love of the highest order, a physical way of entering into the experience of the cross, and an inseparable part of that experience.

The life of the Holy Spirit is revived within us if we follow Him into the wilderness of fasting to face the destruction of the self (at least in part) just as a sheep is led to the slaughter. The secret of this revival of the life of the Spirit within us lies in how well we succeed in attaining this love offered to be slaughtered. This is the first test, if we are to follow the way of the cross to the end.

You know that the effort of fasting is felt primarily by the body, which is the physical area that contains the self where it reveals its nature and desires. Thus, when we fast we exhaust the body, and so, indirectly, subdue the self.[4] If we subdue the self through the subjugation of the body, we have in fact come close to the destruction of the self, at least partially.

So it is that by fasting we fulfill the word of the Lord: "Whoever loses his life for my sake will save it" (Lk. 9:24). Yet I would go back to the word "partially," for we must aim to reach a state of accepting not the partial but the complete annihilation of the self, and this can take place only by an act of deliberate volition. In other words, if we begin with any exercise (such as fasting), which brings us to the partial overcoming of the self, we need to supplement the feeling of satisfaction that comes from accepting this state with an acceptance of the total destruction of the self. This is attained by the mental acceptance of death itself, willingly with no dismay or restraint. But we received the sentence of death in ourselves, that we should not trust in ourselves (cf. 2 Co. 1:9).

When our father Abraham offered Isaac his son, he did so partially with his hands, but totally in purpose. When

[4]Subjugation of the self comes when you undertake some activity which is neither agreeable or desirable. Its attainment is a side-effect of fasting (not the prime motive, which is love).

Abraham proved his willingness to offer Isaac his only son, God did not leave him to carry out the slaughter; when the offering had been only partially made on the physical level, God considered the sacrifice to have been actually carried out. This, and only this, is why God redeemed Isaac with a ram— a symbol of Christ, who was to redeem those souls whose self was destroyed partially by their actions, but wholly in their intentions.

When Abraham offered Isaac his son, he exchanged him, according to the divine plan, for a ram. This signifies the destruction of the body as a ransom for the soul. Likewise, in the test of fasting, or in any act of self-denial based on sacrifice and ransom, we are called upon to have no pity on ourselves and to make the offering of our selves and our bodies a total offering in intention. That is to say, we should be content to accept a sentence of death at any moment, cherishing it deeply within ourselves as a foundation for life.

Yet, God keeps watch to keep destruction from penetrating to the soul. God redeems the soul: "Blessed is God who redeemed my soul" (cf. 2 Sm. 4:9). Christ, blessed be His name, has redeemed our souls, so there is no fear or alarm whatever in facing the experience of self-destruction, as if it would make us search for a ram to offer instead of ourselves. This would mean that our offering was incomplete and our intention weak and hesitant. When intention reaches the stage of complete self-renunciation and consent reaches self-destruction, we see the meek ram fastened with nails to the tree, offered by our compassionate Father at the right time, so that none of those who love Him and believe in Him would perish.

The meaning of all this is that if we offer anything in place of ourselves it is rejected. If we look around in search of a ram to offer instead of the self, we forfeit the promise made forever in Isaac, and even forfeit Christ Himself. For whoever fails to offer his life totally, or is dismayed at the prospect of self-sacrifice, and so of death, finds that his intention retreats and that he rejects death. He becomes evasive and offers an outward sacrifice, such as an act of service or an offering of money, or uses some other stratagem to avoid sacrificing his own self. So he loses his portion in Christ the Redeemer, for Christ redeems from death those who have accepted death.

Therefore, the experience of the destruction of our self must show no self-pity or weakness of faith. It should not be incomplete, nor should we seek to replace it by giving money or anything else in this world, nor even by giving up the whole world, for the soul is more precious than all things. There is nothing that can be offered in exchange for the soul except Christ, may His name be blessed. He alone can be offered; He in condescension and humility through creative Love put a value on His divine soul equal to that of the human soul.

Once more we repeat that Christ, blessed be His name, cannot become a ransom for the human soul unless man offers his soul on the altar of love, in death to the world, making a total offering with all his will, relinquishing himself forever, raising the knife with his own hand in determination and earnest resolve, proving that he has accepted death.

Every test, every battle against the self, and every fast in which man fails to reach this level of self-renunciation (as we see it in the knife raised by Abraham's hand to slaughter Isaac his only son, or in God's abandoning His beloved only Son nailed to the cross) leaves him unworthy of the ransom (Christ) that was prepared by God in exchange for souls offered in this way. A battle is no longer seen as a battle, or fasting as fasting that destroys the self. They are seen, instead, as a caressing of the soul and a strengthening of its power.

The Lord fasted on a high level. He was fulfilling in the flesh and by the flesh what He had already perfected before the incarnation; He "emptied Himself" (Ph. 2:7). He fulfilled this emptying of Himself in many ways, but fasting was the most wonderful, for in fasting He actually sacrificed His body mystically; the fast He undertook and in which He finally experienced extreme hunger and thirst for forty days, proved His clear and earnest intention to make the ultimate sacrifice.

The Lord in fact sacrificed His body before the cross.

When He offered His body to His disciples at the Last Supper, He offered it crucified by an act of His will before it was crucified by the hands of sinners, and sacrificed in intention before it was sacrificed by the rulers. He only said, "Take, eat, this is my body that is offered . . . Take, drink, this is my blood which is shed . . ." (cf. Lk. 22:19,20) on the basis of an inner state at which Christ had already dealt with His soul. The sacrifice and the shedding of His blood had been carried out by His own will and intention, as His fasting bears witness and proves. It was not easy that the Lord, while sitting among His disciples and eating and drinking with them, should say, "This is my body that is offered . . . this is my blood shed . . . ," unless He had actually undergone that sacrifice, even though it were mystically as in fasting.

The Lord crucified Himself for the world before the world crucified Him. He carried out the offering of His body, His self, as a sacrifice on behalf of the world immediately after He was baptized when He was led by the Spirit. He gladly obeyed and went to face the test of fasting. This is the volitional aspect of the cross.

Thus it was that the Lord was careful to institute and celebrate the rite of the eucharist prior to the cross, not after the resurrection, to show that the sacrifice and offering were a free act.

The mystical body that was offered at the Last Supper in the form of bread and wine is the deepest example man has known of the invisible being seen in the visible and the future being actualized in the present. Prophecy in the Old Testament was confined to providing people with a mental image of events in the obscure future, but prophecy as presented by Christ in the New Testament is the good news of the future being fulfilled in the present and a physical receiving of the invisible and the intangible. That is the meaning of "Take, eat . . . Take, drink . . . this is my body . . . this is my blood." This was said a whole day before the crucifixion, but He saw that the coming events were completely in accordance with His will. He saw the cross standing and on it the body being slain and the blood being shed;

He saw Himself content with it all. And so He took bread and filled it with the mystery of the broken body, and wine and filled it with the mystery of the shed blood, and He fed His disciples. They ate from His hands the mystery of His will and drank the mystery of His love, the mystery of His sufferings, the mystery of salvation.

Therefore, when we share in the mystery of the body and the blood in the eucharist, we share not only in the cross, but also in a mystical life poured out and a body that has struggled with severe fasting, deprivation, want, and pain.

If we find ourselves face to face with suffering such as we meet with daily when we bear witness to the truth, we consider ourselves partakers in communion "with those [who were] so treated" (Heb. 10:33). We do not grow faint within ourselves, for the communion in the flesh and blood is an expression that means communion in the whole life of Christ that is fraught with tribulations, fasts, and suffering.

When the Lord Jesus offered His body on Thursday, already sacrificed by an act of will He had made before being crucified on Friday, He drew power from the reality of His own life. Even the cross itself was but an expression of an existing reality, since Christ had crucified Himself for the world before the world crucified Him. It would appear that the crucifixion was the final act of the Lord, but it was in fact the theme of His entire life, begun with the test of fasting, when He sacrificed His body through hunger, and His blood through thirst for forty whole days.

Moses fasted for a similar period of forty days, but this was to prepare him to receive the Commandments and the Law, the written word of God. Elijah fasted for forty days, which was to make him worthy to see and meet with God. The fasting of Moses and Elijah was a profit to them and to mankind. As for the Lord Jesus, He fasted not to receive something but to make a free offering of Himself in an act of will and to manifest the coming sacrifice of the cross.

As for us, we fast not to receive anything or to offer anything, for we have received Christ, and in Him we have already received everything before we fast. In Him we receive everything even before we are born. No offering of ours,

even if we go to our death, is of any avail in removing a
single sin. Nor can our fasting be called redemptive, as if
by sacrificing our bodies and blood by hunger and thirst we
could redeem the smallest soul in all humanity or even ourselves. Why? Because the sin that is within us invalidates the
redemptive act and makes our sacrifice powerless.

What, then, is our fasting?

We fast and offer our bodies as a sacrifice; the outward
form of this is bearing fatigue, but its essence is the intentional acceptance of death, that we may be counted fit to be
mystically united in the flesh and blood of Christ. It is then
that we become, in Christ's sacrifice, a pure sacrifice, capable
of interceding and redeeming.

Fasting, since it is an incomplete sacrifice because of sin,
has to be consummated in Communion, partaking in the pure
body and blood, to become a perfect sacrifice, efficacious in
prayer and intercession. Every Holy Communion Has to be
preceded by fasting, and every fast has to end with Holy
Communion. When we receive Communion in this way it is
right for us to intercede, for our offering and sacrifice are
made perfect. "Pray to receive Communion worthily. Pray
for us and for all Christians" (Coptic Liturgy).

In Lent we prepare ourselves for the Last Supper. We
prepare for two like things coming together. How could those
who do not sacrifice themselves be worthy of Him who
sacrificed His life? If we eat of a sacrificed body and do not
sacrifice our own selves, how can we claim that a union takes
place? The Mystical Supper on Thursday, which is the
intentional acceptance of a life of sacrifice, is but a preparation for accepting sufferings openly, even unto death.

Whenever we eat of the body and drink of the blood, we
are mystically prepared for preaching the death of the Lord
and confessing His resurrection. Every testimony to the death
and resurrection of the Lord carries with it a readiness for
martyrdom. And every martyrdom carries with it a resurrection.

9.

Gethsemane and the Problem of Suffering[1]

Gethsemane is the spot where the great encounter took place, where humankind met with God.

It was not by chance that Jesus sought out a garden at night where He could be distressed and troubled and where His soul became sorrowful with that amazing sorrow unto death. Was it not in the Garden of Paradise that Adam was stripped naked by sin and went out from the presence of God, so that mankind in Adam entered into a state of separation from God and into death?

Even though it is true that humankind experienced a full encounter with God in the birth of Jesus, this was only on the foundation of Jesus' acceptance of a full encounter with us. In Gethsemane, too, we met together with Him; there is no meeting more meaningful than that which takes place in the sharing of suffering, unless it be in the sharing of death itself when we touch immortality.

The suffering that oppresses us in this life, whether in body or in spirit, was plumbed to the depths by Jesus: "My soul is very sorrowful, even to death" (Mt. 26:38). There is no sorrow that can bring the soul to the point of death except the sorrow of shame and sin. It was in Gethsemane that Jesus made the irrevocable decision to accept the shame of humanity. He consented to go to the approaching trial as

[1]From the book *With Christ in His Passion, Death, and Resurrection* by Fr. Matthew the Poor, first published in Arabic in 1961.

a blasphemer and evil-doer, accused of the two sins that are
the basis of all sin.

How did Jesus accept the shame of man?

Christ's acceptance of the shame of man must be counted
a mystery. In order for us to discern it we must drain ourselves of all feelings and emotion; there are few who can
attain to this. Just as the Lord took our nature and was united
to it without its diminishing or changing His divinity, so too
He consented that His body should, in Gethsemane, take on
our stain without being soiled. He did not take sin upon Him
merely in thought, or symbolically or in imagination, for as
the Bible says, "He Himself bore our sins in His body on the
tree" (1 Pt. 2:24).

At this point, who can discern the mystery of Christ and
the heart of redemption?

All we can say is that just as He approached the incarnation and brought it about through His will, so by His will
He bore our sin in His body. And when God wills anything,
it is so. If His hunger, thirst, and weariness are evidence to
us that He was incarnate in a truly human nature, so His
distress and grief and the sorrow of His soul are evidence that
of His free will He mysteriously accepted what mankind was
to lay upon Him on the cross.

Just as the lamb of the sacrifice in ancient times used to
bear a person's sin and die with it for the sinner without the
lamb itself being considered sinful, so the Son of God, the
"Lamb of God" (Jn. 1:29) who takes away the sin of the
whole world, became sin for us, but remained utterly sinless.
"For our sake He made Him to be sin who knew no sin, so
that in Him we might become the righteous of God" (2 Co.
5:21). He remained just as He was, "holy, blameless, unstained, separated from sinners, exalted above the heavens"
(Heb. 7:26).

Just as He, in us, became sin although He remained
utterly sinless, so we, in Him, have become utterly without
sin, although we are sinful human beings. "He took what was

our portion and gave us what was His, so let us praise and glorify and exalt Him."[2]

We met together in Gethsemane and with that the problem of suffering, which has bowed our back and crushed our soul, comes to an end forever.

Before Gethsemane suffering was a punishment

The pain and sadness that follow disasters, injustices, and hardships, and the sickness, humiliation, and degradation that accompany them, remained a question that had no answer, except in the words "sin" and "punishment."

There was no hope in suffering as long as there was no cure for sin. And sorrow was bitter and destructive as long as there was no ransom for punishment.

Moreover, the unjust distribution of suffering caused distress, anxiety, and bewilderment. An innocent child may be the victim of wrong, suffering, and torture just as much as the most evil of men. It may be that good and humble men suffer more than the recalcitrant and profligate, for there is no way to discover any law or principle that governs the distribution of suffering. Why? Because sin ruled over man instead of God, and sin knows no law. The law of sin is injustice; its rule is inequality and its principle is tyranny.

Now if we chose sin by our own desire, could we blame God that we have fallen under sin's oppressive law? So that we would not blame our Creator for the suffering that bears down upon us as a result of the sin we committed by our own capricious will, God sent His Son in a human body to suffer the sufferings of man, though He Himself did not deserve to suffer. In Gethsemane, and after, the Son of God suffered and His soul was sorrowful unto death, and His sweat fell in drops like blood, as though He were bleeding from some hidden wound.

Let us consider this: If a sinful man suffers and is oppressed by a certain amount of pain, it is because this is the law of sin.

[2]Coptic psalmody: Theotokia of Friday.

And if a good man suffers more than an evil man, it is because the law of sin holds sway over them both; in the rule of sin there is no just distribution.

And if an innocent child suffers as adults do, it is because he is a child of sin, born only to injustice and oppression.

But why is it that Christ should bear this overwhelming suffering? Why should His soul grieve with a great sorrow unto death? For He was born of the Holy Spirit and a pure Virgin; He lived without sin and said, "I am the truth" (Jn. 14:6). Must we not therefore understand that Christ deliberately accepted His unjust suffering and consented to bearing the iniquitous sentence "with loud cries and tears" (Heb. 5:7)?

It may be true that there are men who have suffered unjustly and have been penalized more severely than their sins warranted, but what shall we say of Christ? In His suffering He bore all injustice and by the crushing sorrow of His soul He paid the penalty for all sin. As it is said by Isaiah the prophet:

> Surely He has borne our griefs and carried our sorrows; yet we esteemed Him stricken, smitten by God, and afflicted. But He was wounded for our transgressions, He was bruised for our iniquities; upon Him was the chastisement that made us whole . . . All we like sheep have gone astray; we have turned every one to his own way; and the Lord has laid on Him the iniquity of us all. He was oppressed, and He was afflicted, yet He opened not His mouth . . . although He had done no violence, and there was no deceit in His mouth. Yet it was the will of the Lord to bruise Him; He has put Him to grief; when He makes Himself an offering for sin . . . He poured out His soul to death. (Is. 53:4-12)

Then pain became a gift

So it was that God eliminated the oppression of suffering

and its injustice and tyrannical law—not with a message, or a law, or a vision, or an angel, but by coming as a man, bearing that very oppression, and submitting to the law of injustice, being afflicted but not opening His mouth. Christ, by accepting suffering in this way, gave pain itself a greater value, for after being a deserved punishment for sin, it became a sacrifice of love and a work of redemption. From then on suffering was no more bound to sin. Ended was the feeling that tortured man in his heart and conscience that he was under punishment and paying retribution. Such feelings as these would undermine his whole psychological condition and burden him with care, anxiety, and the sicknesses of death, but now, if we are in Christ, we can undergo suffering on the level of His suffering, not as a just consequence of sin, but as a participation in the suffering of love, self-sacrifice, and redemption. Pain, no matter what form it may take, has in Christ become a gift: "Let them thank the Lord for His steadfast love . . . to the sons of men!" (Ps. 107:8).

And a participation in love with Christ

When Christ underwent the appalling suffering even though He did not deserve to bear the least pain, He transformed the meaning of the injustice of suffering. Before, a man who suffered unjustly would raise his eyes to heaven to blame God or ask for mercy, but he would receive no reply, no answer, no consolation; sin had cut the man off from his Creator and had cruelly locked together the suffering man and his offender, driving them together to death and destruction, for that is the way of sin and where it leads. Now the suffering man is forever free from sin in Christ; he sees no injustice in his suffering, no matter how great his pain or how complete his innocence. He sees and feels that his suffering has nothing to do with paying a debt or atoning for a crime, since the severest pain, or indeed all the pain of humanity gathered together, could not atone for even a small sin. Sin is a breach with God and a departure from His presence. Were suffering a punishment and no more, and if we paid the penalty, then who would bring about the reconciliation? Even if we died to pay the price of sin, who would bring us to life again and take us into the presence of God?

But Christ abolished sin, and reconciled and brought us to life. In so doing He broke the fearful link that bound suffering to sin. For suffering is no longer a participation in the sin of Adam, but a participation in the love of Christ.

If we are in Christ, no matter how much we suffer, and no matter how severe our pain, our suffering is in no way related to whether we deserve that pain. Suffering is no longer a penalty for anything, nor is it a means of atoning for anything, or a punishment for anything. It was sin that decreed that suffering should be a form of penalty or atonement or punishment, and Christ eliminated sin after paying its penalty, atoning for it, and bearing its punishment.

It is now therefore as if man suffers for nothing, or for no reason or excuse; this is the type of suffering Christ bore! This is the liturgy of the suffering of love, self-sacrifice, and redemption. This is participation in the divinity, "provided we suffer with Him in order that we may also be glorified with Him" (Rm. 8:17).

And finally, participation in the glory and joys of resurrection

Can we now understand the meaning of the saying, "For it has been granted to you that for the sake of Christ you should not only believe in Him but also suffer for His sake" (Ph. 1:29)? And discern that pain, after being a punishment, has become in Christ a gift? And that the gift of suffering not caused by sin is inevitably a participation in glory?

If we notice the words of James the Apostle, "Count it all joy, my brethren, when you meet various trials" (Jm. 1:2), we discover that any suffering of any kind is unavoidably linked with Christ, and that we must receive it with joyful thanks, knowing that, "as we share abundantly in Christ's sufferings, so through Christ we share abundantly in comfort too" (2 Co. 1:5).

So we no longer suffer for sin, but for Christ. All pain outside of Christ is sin, and the pain of sin is death.

The sufferings of a man who is living with Christ are not counted as the result of sin. They are the sufferings of righteousness; they are joy and peace: "Now I rejoice in my sufferings" (Col. 1:24); they are a participation in the supreme sacrifice of love which Jesus offered through His suffering and perfected by His death: "That I may know Him . . . and may share His sufferings, becoming like Him in His death" (Ph. 3:10).

If we are in Christ, the more our sufferings increase, the more in fact, our participation in this sacrifice increases. The bond is strengthened between us and the resurrection with its joys. Thus it is that the meaning of unjust suffering has been completely reversed; having been violent oppression under the law of sin which held sway over the world, it has now become the measure of a great gift and a mark of worthiness for glory and the joy of the resurrection. "For the law of the Spirit of life in Christ Jesus has set me free from the law of sin and death" (Rm. 8:2). The Apostle Peter also speaks out of his own experience: "For one is approved of if, mindful of God, he endures pain while suffering unjustly" (1 Pt. 2:19).

Thanks be to God the Father and the Lord Jesus. "Let them thank the Lord for His steadfast love . . . to the sons of men" (Ps. 107:8).

All you who suffer, be comforted, for your pain is no longer a result of sin, but a participation in love and in the suffering of Gethsemane.

All you who sorrow and weep, rejoice, for your grief is not unto death; in the sorrow of Christ it is reserved for the resurrection.

10.

The Passion of Jesus Christ in our Life[1]

A new vision of suffering

After Christ had proved His supreme authority over death by raising Lazarus from the dead, and after Mary's anointing Him with precious ointment, which He considered a real unction of the body in preparation for death, Christ marched forward to the cross in order to fulfill the Gospel and to actualize all His precepts and works by facing suffering and voluntary death.

But let us not overlook how the Lord began His seven miracles and how He concluded them (according to the Gospel of John), for they are most strongly linked together.

We know that the first among His signs took place in the house of those who loved Him, among people who were apt to believe in Him. This took place at the wedding of Cana of Galilee where he changed water into good wine in answer to a request by the Virgin Mary, His mother.

Finally, we are also in the house of beloved people— Lazarus, Mary, and Martha—who were the most firm among those who believed in Him. At the pleading of Mary, Lazarus' sister, He restores Lazarus to life. It is here that He manifested His glory, as is recorded in the Gospel. In the first miracle His only objection to the Virgin's pleading was that

---

[1]The first part of this chapter, "A New Vision of Suffering," was published first in 1979. The second part, "Suffering Is Our Path to Glory," appeared in 1968.

131

His hour had not yet come. But by now, after three years or more, the hour had come, leaving no room for any objection against performing miracles. It is here also that the Gospel records for us that He revealed His glory. And this is always the case; Christ finds in no one other than those who believe in Him the most appropriate chances to perform His signs and manifest His glory.

Right after changing water into wine, Jesus began teaching: how to change a person by a new birth from above, from heaven, of water and the Spirit, initiating him into a new eternal life. This Nicodemus could hardly grasp. Similarly, in raising Lazarus from the dead, He performed a conspicuous sign of His ability to raise the dead, to effect total conversion. It is here that the difficulty reached its climax for those who rejected Him. So much was their unbelief that they conspired at that moment to kill both Lazarus and Jesus.

So the pangs of death started quite early before the cross; but what a paradox! The Passion of the Lord began at once, when He openly revealed His real identity. He entered Jerusalem as the King of Israel, and Owner of the Temple, or, according to the prophecies, He who "will suddenly come to His temple" (Ml. 3:1); "But who can endure the day of His coming?" (Ml. 3:2).

Indeed the chief priests and all the teachers of the Law, together with the guardians of holy things and of teaching, could not bear such a spectacle! Not that He entered Jerusalem and the Temple in such glory, but, quite to the contrary, that He came meekly and humbly on a donkey, disappointing their expectations.

It is by absolute rejection, humiliation, and extreme hatred that His Passion began; He came meekly and humbly, which itself was incompatible with the dreams of Israel. In this way has Christ entered from the narrow way. In Him was the prophecy fulfilled: "One abhorred by the nations, the servant of rulers" (Is. 49:7).

Thus begins the way of the cross, right now, for those who cling to truth. It is here that this ever-hateful paradox to authorities appears, hearing the truth from a weakling's mouth.

From now on, the Coptic Church has most wisely set forth Sunday as the beginning of Passion Week, when on that particular day the honor and welcome paid to Jesus reach their zenith, and when the Church cries out, "Hosanna [save us] in the Highest, King of Israel. Blessed is He who comes in the name of the Lord." In the meantime, the Church starts chanting its Psalms in their plaintive tunes and sings the Gospel in a most pathetic melody that wrenches one's heart while the traces of the Oblation are still there on the altar.

Quite amazing! Yet this is the concept of Christ, of the Gospel as the Church is aware of it, a paradox beyond reason, where extreme despondency and grief merge together with utmost joy and hope! The Church is aware that rejecting Christ, causing Him harm, insulting Him, and crushing Him on the cross created ineffable and exalted joy for eternal salvation.

Acceptable suffering

Perhaps the deepest thing fathomed by the Christian in understanding the Passion and crucifixion of Christ is that the cross, to Christ, was voluntary and acceptable: "Shall I not drink the cup that My Father has given Me?" (Jn. 18:11). Thus suffering and the crucifixion were not merely voluntary or acceptable; they had become an aim and end in themselves, which Christ came to fulfill: "For this purpose I have come to this hour" (Jn. 12:27).

This induces us as Christians to interpret suffering this way: the Christian who truly believes in the cross should not abuse his freedom and shun it, for the Christian who has fathomed the depth and mysteries of the cross conceives suffering as part and parcel of his faith, or even a portion of his own which he cherishes and is happy to fulfill, and a goal for which he strikes out fearlessly!

In ecclesiastical tradition, it is stated that when Nero pronounced the sentence of death by crucifixion against Peter when he declared his faith in the crucified God, Peter was sorely afraid. He dodged the guards and fled. The Lord then appeared to him in a vision and asked him, "Where are you going, Peter? Would you like Me to go and be crucified for you once again?" Peter then was extremely ashamed. He then suffered bitterly; how could He do such a shameful deed and betray the cross of his Master? He then returned immediately and surrendered himself to his executioners.

Tradition here adds to our faith an element of extreme importance, that those who evade their cup and portion of suffering is only depriving themselves of their portion in the Suffering of Christ. It is as if they need Christ to be crucified for them anew!

The loving hand presenting the cup of suffering

The eyes of Christ never failed to recognize the hand presenting Him with the cup of suffering. Christ never paid attention to the evil hands bearing the hammer and the nail. Nor did He mind the gruff and spiteful faces of the chief priests shouting, "Crucify Him, crucify Him." Even less so did He regard Pilate as a ruler who could pronounce the sentence of death by crucifixion. Likewise, His ears paid no attention to the insults and gloating words proceeding from the mouths of the malicious and vengeful Pharisees, the keepers of the Law and Sabbaths. His eyes were only fixed on the hand of the Father, which is the sole bearer of hammer and nail. His ears attentively listened to the voice of none but the Father while He pronounced the sentence of scourging and crucifixion. Christ clearly stated to Pilate, "You would have no power over Me unless it had been given you from above" (Jn. 19:11).

Pilate thought it was within his authority to release the Lord and not crucify Him. But it was here that Christ checked him, for this was nothing but sheer delusion. Jesus regulated for him the course of the whole cause, accusation, defense, and jury. Pilate actually articulated what Heaven dictated to him! Regardless of the Synod's fraudulent verdict or the corrupt Roman Law. In fact, the sentence of suffering and death on the cross had been first and last mixed in the cup with love by the Father, who had loved Him before the foundation of the world. This cup was even for the sake of God's love to the world! It was not as bitter as it seemed to be, nor was it mixed with the hatred of the spiteful or the intrigue of hypocrites, as far as outward form is concerned. Rather, it was a select portion that the hand of the Father Himself presented, bearing within it the essence of love, resurrection, and life.

In order to relish such a lofty model, we need but go back to minor ones with their beautiful little crosses. A model of this would be Joseph, the blessed young man who bore no grudge against his brothers who threw him into a well and then sold him for silver, to be taken far away, lonely in exile, to Egypt. He lifted his heart and eyes to God, deeming it his portion that came directly from the hand of God. Joseph did not see his "brother's" treacherous, rough hand that suspended him with ropes in the abyss of the well. Nor did he feel any repulsion toward his brothers while they were being paid the price of his blood when they sold him to the Ishmaelites. In all this he saw nothing but the invisible hand, the hand of God Himself, which weaved all these incidents together. At the end we hear him comforting his brothers when their ignominious deed was revealed, saying, "So it was not you who sent me here, but God. You meant evil against me; but God meant it for good" (Gen. 50:22).

Christ came to elevate such a minor experience and such an individual model to a general course, a divine law, a great redemptive cross, a covenant between God and man. He sealed it with His blood and gave His Holy Spirit as a guarantee. This covenant exists in the presence of the most compassionate hand in the whole world, the hand of God, behind each and every stroke dealt to our earthly tabernacle. It is here that His hand is stretched out to play its role of pure love. The pierced hand of Christ, on which our name was inscribed beforehand, has guaranteed our salvation, and is making out of our daily suffering and pains (which seem to be at random) and out of the persecution of our oppressors and the ingratitude of those who deal with us every day a most exquisite cross bearing for us the seed of Life Eternal

with the sweet savor of Christ—a cross in the likeness of
His cross of glory!

Forgive them

Christ accepted the cup handed to Him by the Father,
fraught as it was with disgrace, scandal, ignominy, and
suffering even unto death. He accepted it as if it were love,
absolute love, void of any doubt or grumbling, or even reproof
or groaning. No stronger evidence could be given for such
acceptance than Christ's words, "Father, forgive them; for
they know not what they do" (Lk. 23:34). These words
Jesus uttered in the last hour when pain reached its climax
and scandal was at its utmost, death being at hand.

If the eyes of Christ had not been fixed upon the hand of
the Father bearing the cup of suffering and death, Christ
could not have overlooked the bitterness surrounding Him,
the foolish hostility, the spite and gloat, the extreme oppression, or all the folly the devil used on the hierarchy, the
elders of the people, and the treacherous disciple.

When Christ commanded us to ask in our daily prayers
for forgiveness of those who have sinned against us, this
commandment did not come out of a vacuum, nor was it like
the orders of the Law, unable as they were to redeem or grant
salvation. Rather, Christ's comandment appeared against the
striking background of the cross, based as it was on obedience to the love of God, a cross which He commanded us to
carry in His wake, in imitation of Him.

Those who are determined to carry the cross of Christ
should first of all not fall under the illusion of the rough
hands that crucify their hopes and feelings. Nor should they
be bewildered at the ill will of those laying in wait for them,
or at the intrigues of the spiteful. They have only to fix their
eyes on the loving and compassionate hand that has laid the
yoke of the cross upon their shoulders, with all the details
that accompanied the crucifixion of Christ as a portion assigned
and specified with utmost accuracy and in accordance with
the dispensation of the divine love that measures everything

by the scale of the glory of Christ. This means that however heavy our cross might be, and however far the enemy (in compliance with evildoers) might go in pressing hard the burden laid upon our feeble shoulders in whatever foolish manner, the divine hand in its turn also measures our due portion in the corresponding weight of glory, in the cross of Christ. This takes place in such a manner that if the veil on our eyes, woven by the enemy against us in such moments, were to be lifted up even for an instant, together with feebleness of the soul, boredom, and afflicted nerves, we would at once realize that the light weight of this cross, together with our slight momentary affliction, have in reality created, by the demonstration of the Spirit, an eternal weight of glory, placed before us in heaven, that could be seen by the spirit in the very depths of the heart—a matter that actually facilitates for us a whole-hearted forgiveness of others, to the point of prayer and love for all those who have sinned against us and have inflicted harm upon us, however great such harm or injury, even unto death!

Life Eternal, with all its resplendent glories, is latent in the mystery of the sweet little cross that the Lord has laid upon our shoulders!

Ongoing hostility toward Christ and His witnesses

No sooner had the outstanding power of Christ appeared, His miracles been manifested, and His conspicuously resplendent deeds and words been spread all over than the chief priests, scribes, and Pharisees, and all those who used religion for earning their livelihood, started first to arouse suspicion, then to attack, then to lay in wait hunting for words and deeds. Finally there was no alternative to the hidden conspiracy, plotting matters in utmost haste, to do away with that alien, lest their prestige be lost and their trade grow listless, as the High Priest himself said.

What must be apparent to our eyes is that the direct cause of their stance against Christ, their resistance and crucifixion of Him could be summed up in one phrase: *The dazzling success of Christ*—His success in elevating the spirits of the people and their understanding of the Law, in infusing joy among people in general, and in particular among the sinners, the discarded, the humiliated, the rejected, the crushed, the sick suffering from hopeless diseases, and those possessed by diabolic powers.

Once again, the success of Christ, His love, His compassion, and His gentleness were the reason for His suffering and crucifixion—as far as the world is concerned. But as for God the Father, the case is utterly to the contrary. In the cross the counsel of the Father together with the consent of the Son in full obedience and contentment had resolved to rescue the world, so that those who believe in Christ and in His passion would not perish. The cross is the new ark which carries all standards; it crosses the deluge of the world and the impending horrors of death up to this moment till it safely conveys its passengers to heaven, the world of everlasting peace.

The same kind of hostility displayed by the powers of darkness and by their prince toward Christ the Savior still exist today, along with the spite of those who crucified Him —be they priests or elders, urged on as they were by personal motives of profit and by their blind fantacism that forged the letter. Such malice, folly, and blind fanaticism still finds a target in anyone bent on witnessing and tracking Christ in his own life.

Suffering is our path to glory

Blessed are those who mourn, for they shall be comforted.
Blessed are the crucified, for they shall be transfigured.
Blessed are those who are totally crushed, for they shall rule.
Blessed are the hungry, for they shall be filled.

All their sufferings will be forgotten and their tears will be wiped away. In their place a light will point to the horrors they underwent and the mystery of the glory that was the result. The greatness of human fortitude will be revealed along with the power of the merciful acts of God. Suffering will be seen to be almost ludicrously light in comparison with the glory that results from it. Everyone will see that suffering was a sacred trap prepared by God to catch us and bring us to glory. The bearing of suffering is more powerful than worship.

One of the saints says that he saw in a vision a group of martyrs more dazzling in glory than the angels who appeared with them. Around the necks of those who had been beheaded he saw garlands of red flowers in the place where the sword had struck, and these shone and sparkled more brilliantly than any other light in the vision.

For Christ, the mystery of the cross is the mystery of His glory. The overwhelming suffering the Lord underwent, His psychological torment at the injustice and crookedness of His trial, the desertion of His disciples, the treachery of Judas, and the knowledge that the high priests had agreed with one of His disciples to put a value of just thirty pieces of silver on His life—all this was a path for Him to leave the world of passing trivialities and enter into the glory of the Father. We in every time and place must tread the same path. The cross with its enormous suffering cannot be compared with the glory it brought forth. The cross did not come by chance into the life of the Lord; He was born for it. "For this purpose I have come to this hour" (Jn. 12:27). Man is born for suffering, and suffering was born for man. But at the same time the cross was not an irrevocable imposition on the Lord. We feel this from His words and are sure of it in view of His holiness and divinity. He made it irrevocable for Himself —"Shall I not drink the cup which the Father has given Me?" (Jn. 18:11)—in order to share with us the inevitability of suffering. God manifested Himself in the person of Christ His Son as one compelled to suffer, in order to make suffering under compulsion equal to suffering by choice, so no one would be deprived of the mercy of God and the cross would be extended to include all who suffer unjustly.

Pain is in itself a great stumbling block to the human mind, which cannot accept pain as a means of acquiring anything good. The mind believes that pain can be removed by knowledge, so people strive in the field of medicine, for example, to abolish pain and bring relief to humanity. Indeed, if we consider carefully all aspects of the educational process, from the alphabet to the building of a rocket, we find that education is basically an attempt to avoid pain and weariness and need.

Pain is therefore a very difficult subject for the mind and is impossible to accept because to accept pain is to cancel out the mind and all mental activity. So the cross is indeed foolishness and a stumbling block to the Greeks—as St. Paul the Apostle says (1 Co. 1:22,23)—a stumbling block to philosophy, which strives to reach God through free Platonic meditation, knowing nothing of sacrifice and believing that pain leads to death. The attempt to attain God through this form of intellectual audacity entered into Christian thought through pagan mysticism and contaminated it. Origen speaks of the possibility of union with God through meditation, making God static and the human mind dynamic; he ties God to a fixed point and has the mind moving towards Him. This is a pagan venture resulting from the lack of a sense of the fatherhood of God, the descent of Christ, the favor of the Holy Spirit, and His entry into the heart of man. The truth lies in quite the opposite direction, for it is we who are always in the static position and God who moves towards us (Thy Kingdom come). The supreme movement of any person is simply to be alert to the movement of God and ready for His coming: "My heart is steadfast, O God, my heart is steadfast" (Ps. 57:7).

If we realize that the cross is the greatest manifestation of the movement of God within visible events since in it God was transfigured for man (more than on Mount Tabor), and that the cross is suffering in its greatest, most oppressive and unjust form, then we must also sense that the cross is, so to speak, the beast of burden upon which God Almighty rode to descend from His dwelling place, where He had been veiled from all eternity, and came to us and took us by the hand. The cross is the supreme power of the dynamism of God, which brought Him down to us and clearly revealed Him.

That is to say that suffering, from a physical point of view, is negative and confirming, but in its spiritual essence is an incomparable movement!

We remain at a spiritual standstill, unable to proceed in our return to God with Christ until we take up the cross. Suffering brings us into the mystery of the cross, the mystery of the divine movement, so that we no longer stand still like one dead, but are drawn to Christ, guided and led on from suffering until we attain the Father, borne on our cross, following in the way of Christ.

It is impossible for us to move toward God by mental effort, for the mind, no matter how far it progresses in meditation, can only discover God and His light and love. This brings the mind happiness, but then it falls away. True movement toward God is in Christ, for He is the Son of God who comes to us on the cross, and on the cross we follow Him back to the Father.

He says, "Apart from Me you can do nothing" (Jn. 15:5). He says this not because He would tyrannically override our will, nor because we are unable to attain knowledge, for He taught us all we need to know. It is because He alone, as the Son, has within Him the power to move toward God the Father. Christ carries in Him the power of two movements, the movement of God the Father toward us and our movement toward the Father.

The first is natural and essential, having its being in the mystery of His love for His creation. The second is acquired through the cross,[2] that is, through the sacrificial suffering

[2]Christ alone has the power to move toward the Father because He is the only-begotten Son of God who is of one essence with the Father. He is ever in the bosom of the Father and turned toward the Father. (The Greek word πρός which is used in the first verse of the Gospel of John and is usually translated "with," "the Word was with God," also means "toward," that is "the Word was toward God."

This power was natural in Christ before the incarnation and the cross, but in order to bear humankind, being dead, and bring it to the Father, He had, after taking flesh and becoming a man, to undergo sacrificial suffering, so that He might take us up into the presence of the Father. Thus Christ acquired for us through the cross a power for our good, that is, the power to bring sinful humanity toward the Father. "For it was fitting that He, for whom and by whom all things exist, in bringing many sons to glory, should make the pioneer of their salvation perfect through suffering" (Heb. 2:10).

that was prepared to bear lifeless humankind and raise it up.

And Christ has filled us with the mystery of these two powers: the power of love and the power of the cross, that is, suffering. By our receiving these two powers Christ works in us mystically so that we can move through Him and with Him until we attain the Father. Then through these two powers and in Him, there is the greatest mystery, which is the mystery of union with God.

I commit you to the providence of God's great loving care that makes use of all ages and times and events, and of everything that befalls us or that we attain, to perfect His plan of salvation for all humankind.

Be strong.

11.

Resurrection and Redemption in the Orthodox Concept

Great is the Church's jubilation when it celebrates in the Easter season the resurrection of Christ from the dead, repeating the words *"Christos Anesti."* For the Church these words mean that redemption is accomplished and that it has become a right of all sinners to receive with faith the bond of freedom from the captivity of sin and death and to accept the call to eternal life.

In order to acquire a faith of such strength we have to penetrate the depth of the Church's faith that closely ties together the mystery of the Last Supper (Thursday evening), the mystery of the crucifixion (Friday), and the mystery of the resurrection (dawn of Sunday).

During the Supper of Thursday evening the Lord for the first time revealed the meaning and reality of the forthcoming crucifixion he had often talked about as mere suffering and death. Now suddenly He explained quite briefly and mystically that He would give Himself as a sacrifice on behalf of the world, and that this self-sacrifice would be offered complete to the Father just like the Passover offering, a broken body for them to eat and shed blood for them to drink for the remission of sins and for life eternal.

What astonished the disciples at the Supper, and still astonishes the whole world, is that Christ was not theoretically explaining how He would be slain on Friday, but He was anticipating events. A full day before the crucifixion He offered

Himself actually slain to His disciples, not as a mere act of intention or illustration but as an actual act of breaking, slaying, and shedding blood more deeply and clearly than in the events on Friday on the cross, so that all the mysteries of Christ's self-sacrifice on the cross on Friday—impossible for any human to perceive or comprehend—were revealed by Him at the Thursday Supper and illustrated to His disciples.

After breaking the bread and mixing the wine Christ offered both to His disciples, not merely as a representation or symbol of the breaking of His body and the shedding of His blood on the cross: "This is My broken body, this is My shed blood." Here Christ performed an act of voluntary death through an ineffable mystery.

He then declared the cause of breaking or slaying, "on your behalf," then the purpose, "for the remission of sins."

Above all He ordered them *to eat and drink of it*, not as bread yet unbroken or wine yet unmixed, but as the actually slain body, demonstrating that the mystery of Friday was present before them as a real divine Passover, that the death on the cross on Friday would not only be an offering to the Father for the sins of the world, but a sacrifice of love and a perpetual Supper in which the whole world could share. In this way Christ clearly and openly revealed that His self-sacrifice on the cross was an atonement sacrifice that He would offer before God the Father not only as a spontaneous act on behalf of the people, but a sacrifice of personal love where atonement would not be accomplished except by actually sharing it. In the mystery of the Supper, Christ explained that perfect actual sharing in the belief in the crucified Christ as a sacrifice of salvation and remission of sins must be accomplished by actual partaking of the body and the blood in accordance with the mystery perfected in the Thursday Supper. Only in this way can we come to atonement, forgiveness, and union with Christ for extension in life eternal.

The Orthodox Church thus believes that the Thursday Supper, which is the Eucharist, and the Friday crucifixion are one and the same mystery, and also that the one cannot be comprehended without the other, nor can the secret of the power of one be attained without the other. Love was the

motive for them both. St. John says of Jesus when He sat at
Supper before the feast of the Passover: "When Jesus knew
that His hour had come to depart out of this world to the
Father, having loved His own who were in the world, He
loved them to the end" (Jn. 13:1). It is for this love that
Jesus died and rose from the dead.

Again, a deep look into the mysteries of the Supper will
reveal that the declaration of the mystery of resurrection
within the declaration of the mystery of His death was quite
clear. While Christ offered Himself to His disciples by saying,
"Take, eat my broken body, and drink my shed blood," He
offered body and blood with His own hands, alive and not
dead. Christ in the Thursday Supper was at once slain and
risen, dead and alive. It is an amazing mystery with which
Christ could strongly yet mystically unveil the resurrection
inherent in the imminent death on the cross on Friday: "I
am the first and the last, and the living one: I died, and
behold I am alive for evermore" (Rv. 1:17,18).

Thus we can perceive the magnitude of the Eucharist
accomplished by Christ in the Thursday Supper and by the
Church to this day, the mystery that explains not only the
secrets of the crucifixion on Friday but also of the Christ dead
and alive and of redemption in its entirety, considering that
the death suffered by Christ was but a voluntary and atoning
love sacrifice signifying the power of death on behalf of the
others and the power of resurrection along with the others.
Consequently it is a sacrifice capable of giving eternal life,
instead of death, for the sins of the past through the mystery
of the communion accessible to all and conveyed by this
sacrifice, a communion in the body and blood of the slain
and risen Christ.

The Church realized that death on the cross was both a
living and a life-giving sacrifice, atoning and raising from
the dead. All this was comprehended by the Church through
the mystery of the Supper. Here again the Church goes back
to the secrets of the Last Supper and unveils essential facts
related to the events of Friday.

For Christ the cross was not, as the high priests mistook
it, an instrument of torture and death to a sinner and

blasphemer ("Crucify Him, crucify Him!"), but in the mind
of the Father and in the depth of Christ it was an instrument
of self-sacrifice stemming from a sweeping, atoning love.
The Church concluded this from the mystery of the Last
Supper and from the discourses of Christ in the Gospel of St.
John. Did He not foretell the kind of death He would suffer?
"Greater love hath no man than this, that a man lay down
his life for his friends."

Thus through resurrection, the cross was transformed from
being an instrument of retribution and death in the hands of
the crucifers to being an effective instrument of divine love
in the hands of the good Shepherd, who redeemed His sheep
and who today also follows the lost sheep to the end of the
earth. What place in the world is without a raised cross, a
cross that seeks sinners to restore them to the Father's fold?
The cross has become an instrument of joy for all those who
comprehend within it the mystery of forgiveness, the mystery
of divine love, "for He loved me and gave Himself for my
sake."

So Christ died only to offer Himself as the sacrifice of all
sinners in the world, and through this sacrifice to give His
broken body and shed blood to every person just as He did
on Thursday, so that He might eat and drink forgiveness,
resurrection, and everlasting life.

Christ still practices in every Church and among His beloved people the mystery of His Supper. Just as He did at
the Thursday Supper He offers on every altar with His own
hands His body and blood to communicants for remission of
sins and for life eternal; the Eucharist has come to convey to
us all the Thursday Supper power of infinite love, the power
of the pains endured by the flesh on the cross, and the power
of the resurrection in which the body rose and left the grave
empty.

But let us not forget that these deep meanings treasured
in the mystery of the Supper and all the light emanating from
them to reveal the glory of the cross were not grasped by the
disciples until they were sure that Christ had risen. During
the Supper the disciples understood nothing at all of what the
Lord said and explained. The words Christ spoke about the

new covenant, the shed blood, the remission of sins, and the eternal life conveyed no sense to them; the Gospel says, "their hearts were filled with sorrow." When the hour came and steps were taken to arrest Jesus, and when they were faced with the publicity of the accusations and the declaration of the crucifixion, they panicked and fled, and some denied Him in spite of all that Christ had told them beforehand. It is as if Christ had not celebrated the Eucharist, or washed their feet or talked about His death for at least six hours at a time (according to St. John), or about His resurrection, His return, or His sending the Comforter to them, or how He would not leave them comfortless and how He would see them again and they would rejoice. All this vanished in face of their fear of violence, the appearance of the high priests' soldiers, and the proceedings of the arrest.

Resurrection in the Church's theology on the concept of the cross—as a voluntary self-sacrifice for the atonement of the sins of all the world—stands both as a foundation and a summit. The mystery of resurrection as a tangible reality of faith was like a heavenly glorious light which, when it entered the hearts of the disciples, transformed all the humiliating and painfull sorrows of the cross into honor, triumph, and glory. Death became redemption, the grave turned from the pit of death into the fountain of life.

It is not without reason that St. Paul said, "And if Christ has not been raised, your faith is futile and you are still in your sins" (1 Co. 15:17). What is more important in the theology of the Church, which actually believes that He has risen, is this: "If Christ be raised and His resurrection became a reality within us, then our faith is true and we are no longer in our sins." This means that Christ's resurrection in the flesh on the third day has become the fundamental and effective power for the forgiveness of sins. Consequently, resurrection in the Church's view is the basis of the concept of atonement. Therefore we cannot say that Christ's death by itself meant paying the price of our sins and appeasing God in order to remove His wrath from us. It is the resurrection that gave the death of Christ this force, atonement, and reconciliation.

When we consider the joyful song of the Church *"Christos Anesti,"* we realize the reason for this overwhelming joy that annihilated all the sorrows and agonies of the cross, all the pains of sin and death. For if Christ has risen, then our faith is true and we are no longer in our sins. His cross was not an ignominy but a glory. If the body we eat and drink is the body of His crucifixion, it is also the body of His resurrection, and we are partakers in the self-same resurrection and life eternal.

Christ's resurrection turned the disgrace and curse of the cross into grace, salvation, and glory, and made the broken body and the shed blood not only alive but also life-giving. Moreover, if death was paid as a price for our sins, resurrection increased this price by making it openly and permanently acceptable both in heaven and on earth.

Our dire need is for a resurrection that has the same strength and revelation as that given to the disciples on the third day, that it may correct all our erroneous concepts of fear of suffering and the cross, and become a beginning for our faith and a force from which we draw our ability not only to comprehend the power of Christ's cross to forgive our sins, but also to endure the same agonies of the cross with all joy. It would no longer be an agony but a communion in glory, as St. Paul discovered: "[If] we suffer with Him in order that we may also be glorified with Him" (Rm. 8:17).

In the doctrine of the Orthodox Church, resurrection has come to be the foundation of the act of redemption that was latent in the heart of Christ from the very beginning. Redemption did not mean merely that Christ should pay the price of our sins or remove the wrath of God from the reprobate who were enslaved to sin. To Christ redemption meant in the first place something beyond forgiveness and reconciliation—to restore the love and eternal life we had lost through transgression and separation from God. This was originally implied in the concept of incarnation as understood by the Fathers of the Church, such as St. Athanasius who says: "The Word became human that we might become gods in Him" (that is, partakers of the divine nature).

The aim of incarnation, therefore, in the view of the

Orthodox Church Fathers[1] never stopped short at the atonement of the cross or redemption by blood, but always proceeded further to resurrection for the renewal of man as the ultimate end of incarnation. Why? Because man would not stop at falling into sin or breaking with God and incurring divine wrath, even if his sins were remitted. Because man lost his original gifts and the image of God was distorted in him, he finally lost his power to know and love God, and consequently to return to life with God through purgation, knowledge, and instruction. To reconcile ourselves with God and to return to our original state is not a question of repaying the debt of our sins; there must be a re-creation of the self. This we hear from Christ Himself when He approached this problem with Rabbi Nicodemus: "Unless one is born anew, he cannot see the Kingdom of God" (Jn. 3:3).

The resurrection of Christ from the dead in the same body in which He had died gives the practical and divine answer to the manner of our new birth as a new creation. The power of Christ to restore life to man through his resurrection has been the greatest hope of the Church ever since the day of resurrection. Through His resurrection, alive and victorious not only over sin but also over death, Christ once and for all opened the door for our return to the Kingdom of God, that is to eternal life, after He had paid the price of our sins on the cross.

Thus the resurrection of Christ reveals to us the stronger motive behind the cross. Behind the sacrifice that was accomplished with the full consent of the Son and the pleasure of the Father who bruised Him with grief, there were paternal mercy and supreme affection from the Lord Jesus toward sinners and humanity at large, not merely for the forgiveness of their sins, but for their re-creation in Him and in His Spirit that He might present them with Him in His love to the Father after being washed in His blood, and present them in His rising and sitting on the right hand of the Father, that they might be without blemish before God the Father

---

[1]Some scholars concerned with contrasting the saints of the West and those of the East say that the former always bear the stigmata of the cross, while the latter always shine with the transfiguration of the resurrection.

in love, and be a new creation drawing its very breath from the Spirit of God, beloved like Him. Or in the words of Christ Himself: "The love with which Thou hast loved Me may be in them." (Jn. 17:26).

The doctrine of the Orthodox Church, in emphasizing the love of God as a basic motive, extends from the cross to the resurrection and ascension, and even to the entry into the holy of holies and the sitting on the right hand of the Father in order to ensure the consummation of redemption. Therefore the Orthodox Church believes that redemtpion continued even after Christ's entrance into the higher holies—"entered once into the Holy Place . . . thus securing an eternal redemption" (Heb. 9:12).

Christ is still alive, and even after He died for us and justified us with His blood He still intercedes for us before God the Father by the boldness of the love with which He accomplished the redemption, so that no wrath or blame may befall us on account of our ignorance and daily transgression: "but God shows His love for us in that while we were yet sinners Christ died for us. Since, therefore, we are now justified by His blood, much more shall we be saved by Him from the wrath of God" (Rm. 5:8,9).

How erroneous we are when, after this wonderful and glorious salvation has been accomplished in all its stages, we sever the cross from the resurrection, considering the cross in our heart and mind as an area of grief and disgrace which we shun and apprehend while making resurrection a cherished exultation and glory. For is not resurrection the price of the cross and the cross the price of resurrection, and were not the two one glory for Jesus and for us? Was not the cross in the eyes of the Father the true glory of Christ while He was hanging on it and beset with disgrace? Did not Jesus Himself reveal this fact in His prayer to the Father when Judas went to carry out His act of betrayal and when Christ realized that the hour of the cross was at hand? "After receiving the morsel, He immediately went out: and it was night. When He had gone out, Jesus said, 'Now is the Son of man glorified, and in Him God is glorified; if God is glorified in Him, God will also glorify Him in Himself, and glorify Him at once' "

(Jn. 13:30-32). That was the halo of glory that Jesus saw beforehand surrounding Him on the cross and in the resurrection in the same measure.

With its keen theological sense the Orthodox Church comprehends that Christ subjected Himself to death but did not come under its sway. Resurrection was immanent in Him, and He consented to crucifixion only in the measure of His own commitment to His love for sinners. "Greater love hath no man than this, that a man lay down his life for his friends" and His obligation of obedience to the Father "became obedient even unto death, the death of the cross."

This is why Scripture and the prophets stated that it was not possible that He should be held by the grave. Resurrection here came to emphasize His voluntary death.

How often Jesus alluded to this subtle and basic point. "I have power to lay it down, and I have power to take it again" (Jn. 10:18). "Shall I not drink the cup which My Father has given me?" (Jn. 18:11). "For this I have come into the world" (Jn. 18:37). When Pilate wanted to show his superiority over the "king of the Jews," that he could crucify Him or set Him free, Christ immediately objected: "You would have no power over Me unless it had been given you from above" (Jn. 19:11).

Pilate accomplished his task, gratified the high priests, and crucified Jesus just as they wished and as the devil wished, so that the cross might be a shame upon Christ and a final retribution, and that the Jews might do away with Him once and for all. But through His triumph and resurrection from the dead the Lord foiled all that they contrived with the prince of this world and the power of darkness; the Lord reversed the situation, so that to Christ and to every believer the cross became glory and peace, and to the devil and all the haters of Christ's name it became disgrace and horror.

Resurrection seated Christ in the heavens as King of kings, and Lord of lords, and Master of all ages, and made the death of Christ a propitiation not only for the remission of sins and the reconciliation of the world to God, but a renewal of human creation and a radical change in the very nature of humanity from a physical life in the flesh to one in the Spirit, to prepare the corruptible to be made incorruptible and the mortal to be made immortal. According to St. John in the Revelation, "He that is holy let him be holy still" (cf. Rv. 22:11).

Our life in Jesus Christ is henceforth written for us in heaven in the newness of the spirit, that we may reign with Christ. All the daily deeds of the Church have become known to and read by all heavenly beings, because Christ, who sits at the right hand of power in heaven, is also the King of saints for the heavenly Church, and He is here the head and the bridegroom of the Church on earth, just as St. Paul says: "That through the Church the manifold wisdom of God might now be made known to the principalities and powers in the heavenly places. This was according to the eternal purpose which He has realized in Christ Jesus our Lord" (Eph. 3:10,11). Whether in the sacrament of baptism, where death with Christ and resurrection with Him are accomplished to obtain the new birth that qualifies us to enter the Kingdom of heaven and behold it from now, or in the sacrament of Eucharist, where the body of Christ is revealed, the Spirit descends and believers partake of the oblation, declaring His death and confessing His resurrection in preparation for sharing in His resurrection.

Whenever the Church sings the words *"Christos Anesti"* (Christ is risen) the echoes of their response resound in the heavens in the mouths of the saints, *"Alithos Anesti"* (*Verily He is risen*).

12.

Between the Resurrection and the Ascension

There were forty days after the resurrection when Christ was with His disciples. "To them He presented Himself alive after His passion by many proofs, appearing to them during forty days, and speaking of the Kingdom of God" (Ac. 1:3).

This definite period of time when Christ lived on earth in the body with which He passed through death and the tomb and rose alive may be considered the greatest and most precious gift Christ granted to our human nature. The posibility of resurrection from the dead and of a new life in a body free of suffering, death, and corruption was not originally available to the human nature. We know that man had become dead by nature after sin had expelled him from the paradise of life with God, and even though individuals were sometimes raised from the dead at God's command, they were raised to die again, like Lazarus. That we should rise to live forever with God in a body that would neither perish nor be defiled nor fade away is Christ's supreme and indescribable gift, granted to us when He rose with the body He had taken from us.

So it is that everyone who believes in the resurrection of Christ has an automatic faith in his own resurrection also, for faith in the resurrection is itself resurrection, because Christ gives all that is His to all who believe.

But how do we actually attain to the indwelling of the

Spirit of the resurrection and hold in our hands, or rather in our hearts, in earnest the everlasting life? Or, in other words, how can we live now in the Spirit of the resurrection, as if we were risen from the dead with Christ, and have confidence that neither death nor suffering nor any of the affairs of the present life have power over us? Or we may ask the question even more strikingly: how can a person live out of his own deathlessness? How can a man live through Lent not simply as forty days in the liturgical cycle, but as an experience of life completely free of the fear of death and its power, a post-resurrection life, a life that prepares one for ascension?

It is not within our own power to reply to this question. We must go back to the Gospel. The Gospel of John says:

> On the evening of that day, the first day of the week, the doors being shut where the disciples were, for fear of the Jews, Jesus came and stood among them and said to them, "Peace be with you." When He had said this, He showed them His hands and His side. Then the disciples were glad when they saw the Lord. Jesus said to them again, "Peace be with you. As the Father has sent me, even so I send you." And when He had said this, He breathed on them, and said to them, "Receive the Holy Spirit. If you forgive the sins of any, they are forgiven; if you retain the sins of any, they are retained." (Jn. 20:19-23)

All that Christ could do for His disciples, that they would believe in His resurrection, was to show them His hands pierced by the nails, and His side wounded by the spear. For the disciples, even for Thomas the greatest doubter among them, this was quite enough to give them faith in the resurrection, but it was not enough, even with their faith, to give them the Spirit and power of the resurrection. In order for us to believe in something beyond the bounds of knowledge, imagination, and experience, such as the resurrection from the dead, we must have evidence, but in order for us to receive what is beyond our nature and experience, beyond our perception and powers of logic, that is to attain to the power and nature of the resurrection, we must be granted a spiritual gift. And so it was that Christ, after giving His disciples proof of His resurrection so they would believe and rejoice, we find that He comes toward them and breathes upon them to bestow upon them what is beyond their own nature and capabilities, the power of the resurrection itself. This is not simply resurrection from the dead, but resurrection in the Spirit of God with a new nature for man, that prepares him for a new and spiritual life, a life in the Spirit of God with God, where sin and death have no power and where there is no subjugation to ignorance or suffering.

Christ's breathing His Spirit upon the disciples reminds us of God's breathing upon Adam at his first creation: "Then the Lord God formed man of dust from the ground, and breathed into his nostrils the breath of life; and man became a living being" (Gn. 2:7). In both cases the breathing is creative and life-giving: The first breathing is a physical creation to a temporal earthly life. The second breathing is a spiritual creation to an everlasting heavenly life.

Adam received the first breathing and by it became the head of the whole human creation, from whom sprang the whole sequence of human life on earth; this breathing has retained its efficacy in the Adamic nature up to the present time.

The disciples, united in faith, received the second breathing from Christ as the Church, and so Christ became, for the Church, the source of the new spiritual creation, and this breathing of His has remained for the Church the source of a new, heavenly eternal life.

The Apostle Paul makes a clear comparison between these two lives:

The first man Adam became a living being; the last Adam [i.e. Christ] became a life-giving spirit. But it is not the spiritual which is first but the physical, and then the spiritual. The first man was from the earth, a man of dust; the second man is from heaven. As was the man of dust, so are those who are of the dust; and as is the man of heaven, so are those who are of heaven. Just as we have borne the image of the man of dust [i.e. Adam], we shall also bear the image of the man of heaven [i.e. Christ]. (1 Co. 15:45-49)

So the breathing of Christ constituted a new creation of the Adamic nature, bequeathing to it a new spiritual nature not originally its own, granting it the potential of resurrection from the dead and everlasting life with God. Christ is here to be considered a new Father of man, for He begot him anew by His Spirit after his physical birth and gave him a new life, which becomes active and apparent after or beyond the earthly life. It begins after death with resurrection, but resurrection begins mystically now, when we receive after our physical birth a new birth of water and the Spirit and receive the Spirit of the resurrection that the Church breathes into our being.

We have now experienced both births, and both lives are at work in us, life upon life. The spiritual began after the physical, but one is decreasing in order little by little to give way to the other. "Though our outer nature [the physical] is wasting away, our inner nature [the heavenly] is being renewed every day" (2 Co. 4:16). But the point to note here is that while the physical life inevitably and automatically dwindles, whether we wish it or not, we find that the spiritual life, or the resurrection nature, only gains sway in us by our will and desire. This is why Christ, when He breathed the Holy Spirit upon His disciples so that He might endue them with the nature and power of the resurrection, said to them, "Receive the Holy Spirit" (Jn. 20:22). The verb "receive" is here dependent on the extent of a person's readiness and desire. Christ does not grant the Holy Spirit to our nature automatically or mechanically. Our human nature receives the gift of eternal life and the nature of the resurrection according to the depth of striving, desire, and will in the whole soul and heart and mind.

The first breathing at the physical creation was received with no response of the human will. It was given generally and so human life became the rightful possession of all who had a human body. The second breathing at the spiritual creation was received joyfully by only the disciples out of the thousands and millions of the human race. The disciples are therefore counted as the firstfruits of the Spirit. But note that the Gospel says, "The disciples were glad when they saw the Lord" (Jn. 20:20). Here it is the joy of faith in the resurrection of Christ that prepared the disciples to receive the breathing of the Spirit of the resurrection.

So the Spirit and nature of the resurrection are not granted in a general way to every man whether he wills it or not. Those who believe and rejoice at the resurrection of the Lord are those who are called to receive the Spirit of the resurrection. Joy is always the greatest evidence of the readiness of the will, whether it be the will to rise from the dead or the will to live with Christ, and this will is not a mere wish or dream or subject of meditation, but labor and striving and practical action. "If then you have been raised with Christ, seek the things that are above" (Col. 3:1).

This being so, our daily supplications and strivings and the source of our joy are true evidence of our position vis-à-vis the resurrection. This means that we must every day, or rather every hour, conform those things in which we rejoice with our own will to the demands of life with Christ, which is the resurrection life, so that we may effectively receive the breathing of the Holy Spirit toward the continuous renewal of our nature.

The question now arises: how do we begin now to live a post-resurrection life, an eternal life with God, while we still live in a body crushed under the weight of sin? Is it not certain and inevitable that death will rule over the body through sin?

The answer comes from the Gospel, for we find that Christ, after He breathed the Spirit of the resurrection upon His joyful disciples, immediately said to them, "If you forgive the sins of any, they are forgiven; if you retain the sins of any, they are retained" (Jn. 20:23). Here for the first time in the history of mankind, sin comes under the power of man, who had himself formerly fallen under the power of sin. The breathing of the Spirit bestowed by Christ to His disciples here clearly has power to renew the very nature of humanity.

We witness here a profound and portentous upheaval in the life of man.

This new power, which we received by the breathing of the Holy Spirit from the mouth of Christ, clearly and surely reveals that the disciples had actually received resurrection, though mystically and invisibly, for who can forgive sin who is dead or under the power of death? If the disciples had received power to forgive people's sins, it must surely mean that by the breathing of the Holy Spirit, which they received from the mouth of Christ, they destroyed the power that sin had over them, and so overcame the power of death itself. That is, they rose from the dead, spiritually and supremely victorious. And this is not all, for by that Holy Spirit, who took up His dwelling in them, they became able to destroy the power of sin wielded over others too, and consequently the power of death. That is, by their resurrection in Christ, they were able to impart the Spirit of the resurrection to others if they were worthy, "If you forgive the sins of any, they are forgiven; if you retain the sins of any, they are retained" (Jn. 20:23).

So we see that the relationship between the Spirit of the resurrection and human life beyond the power of sin and death becomes a reality in the mystery of forgiveness, which is a mystery of great delicacy and depth. It is the mystery of the life of Christ in action after His resurrection from the dead, who by His death trampled down death and bestowed everlasting life on those in the tombs.

But is there a relationship between Christ's breathing the Holy Spirit upon the disciples after the resurrection and the coming of the Holy Spirit on the Day of Pentecost? The relationship between these two events is a strong one, and each is linked with the other. The breathing of Christ upon the disciples granted them resurrection and everlasting life, and so human nature attained to the power of resurrection from the dead and became the abode of everlasting life. The descent of the Holy Spirit at Pentecost imparted to human nature a spiritual power from on high that would bind and unite all people to one another through the Holy Spirit. This unity might come about through a spiritual word, a moving of the heart, secret acts of service, wonders or miracles, or an attractive and effective living example. The whole object was to form an integral human organism united with Christ and by Christ, by which human nature as a whole might be prepared, as the Church, for life with Christ in heaven.

So the breathing of the Holy Spirit upon the disciples after the resurrection was to grant to human nature the Spirit and power of the resurrection, while the descent of the Holy Spirit upon the disciples after the ascension was to impart to humanity the Spirit and power of the ascension. This is why Christ rose, as one first-born, from the dead, and then ascended into heaven and entered into the holy places as our forerunner. For if Christ had not risen with our body, we could not have risen and man could have known nothing of eternal life. And if He had not also ascended into heaven with our body, it would never have been possible for man to ascend into heaven, even if he rose from the dead. So Christ grants these two powers, of resurrection and ascension, through the Holy Spirit, who takes what is Christ's and gives it to us (cf. Jn. 16:14). This is why the Apostle Paul confirms with certitude that God "raised us up with Him, and made us sit with Him in the heavenly places" (Eph. 2:6).

We have now risen with Christ and we live out our resurrection by the breathing of the Holy Spirit. If the Spirit of Pentecost has descended upon us too, we are also ready for our ascension, and nothing keeps us from heaven except our awaiting the coming of Him who is even now at the doors. "I will come again and will take you to Myself" (Jn. 14:3).

13.

The Ascension of Christ

Let us rejoice in the feast of the ascension at which Christ seated us with Him in heaven and prepared for us the happy abode that He had formerly promised, on the right hand of power in the highest, for we became forever reconciled in Christ with the Father and preserved by the grace and mercy of the Almighty. Unlike the first Adam who dwelt merely in a paradise with trees and fruits and was visited by God from time to time, we in our beloved Redeemer—*the second Adam* —abide always with God. Though we are now exiled from our heavenly home, slightly suffering so our faith can be justified and so we can be worthy of this splendid portion, we live by faith as though we were permanently settled in heaven with the hope poured in us by Christ and the love that turns pain into pleasure and invisible into visible through our inner vision, patiently and gratefully expecting the moment of union when we enjoy beholding the face of our beloved Christ that will never be taken away from us.

It was the pleasure of Christ, before He went off to the Father, which He prayed for (cf. Jn. 17), so we would be where He abides forever, so we could behold His glory and live in it. After His ascension this glory became a living reality, which St. Stephen the martyr witnessed with his own eyes and after seeing it readily quit his earthly tabernacle, beholding with the certitude of faith and sight the place prepared for him by Christ, a wonderful house, not made with hands, eternal in the heavens, the body of Christ which is all-encompassing.

We now eat His body and drink His blood with closed eyes. We cannot see the splendor of this body or the glory of this blood without being terrified, without falling on our faces and being speechless receiving the awesome live coal of divinity. But why can we not see ourselves united with this body in the full light of divinity, and the blood of Christ permeating through us, transmitting to us the Spirit of divinity and pouring it into our being, so that we can become kings and priests to God His Father and reign with Him in the heritage of the boundless sonship to the Father?

This is why St. Paul urges us with a mystical persistence intelligible only to those who by the Spirit are initiated into the secret of divine presence: "If then you have been with Christ, seek the things that are above, where Christ is" (Col. 3:1), which means that resurrection alone is not sufficient. After the resurrection there are the glories of living in the divine presence where with us Christ has sat on the right hand of the Father at the disposal of those who love Him and cannot endure living without Him. Wherever Christ is we have the right to be. This claim is in the very nature of Christ's claim and pleasure, for we earned this right by virtue of our humanity with which He gladly and lovingly united, promising never to forsake or forget it, not even for one moment or for the twinkling of an eye.

To seek those things that are above where Christ sits is to seek perpetual being in the presence of God, which became for us an eternal right in Christ that we now claim persistently and with tears. Once we have possessed it, it cannot be taken away from us, for it is our portion reserved for us in heaven, which is not defiled through our infirmity and does not fade away through the decay of our carnal being.

To live in the presence of God, conscious of the union with Christ that He freely accomplished in us and for us, is the secret of happiness provided by Christ for us amid the sorrows of the world and despite the helplessness of humanity and its tragic failure. This consciousness should give us an inner peace that transcends the mind with all its troubles and weaknesses.

But this sense of being in the presence of God is not mere

fun to be enjoyed. Rather, it is prayer in the fullness of its warmth, tranquility, and sobriety, the perfect prayer in which the body calms down, the soul finds rest, and the spirit rejoices in the remembrance of the Trinity, the glorification of the Father, the reiteration of the Savior's name, and the ceaseless call of the Holy Ghost with hope and boldness derived from the cross and the shed blood.[1]

We are bound to groan within ourselves because of the burden of the flesh, which is like a tent torn apart by wild winds, and we yearn to put on over it clothing from heaven. But this is not possible, since we must first take it off so we may put on Christ and abide in Him uninhibited, for the corruptible cannot inherit incorruptibility. Hence will our prayers remain mixed with tears, and will our joy of abiding in the divine presence be tinged with groans of grief on account of our inability to put on the heavenly raiment here and now. But we trust that just as we have put on the earthly so shall we put on the heavenly and never be found naked of divine grace, because He Who created us has Himself recreated us and prepared us for renewal in the fullness of holiness and righteousness of God.

Therefore we should admit our dire destitution, even though all the wealth of the Son's heritage was decreed and bequeathed to us. For this world of deceit and fraud is no place of riches for us. Here there is no permanent city for us, no lasting home, no honor, no renown, no name or true comfort. We rather seek the world to come where there is no deceit or shadow of turning. In this spirit St. Paul urges us to "seek those things which are above." Can a man seek those things while he seeks things that are on this earth and still covets what is in the hands and mouths of others? Either

---

[1]The relationship between humanity and the life-giving Spirit became possible through the redemptive sacrifice of Christ: "It is to your advantage that I go away . . . if I go, I will send Him [the Comforter] to you" (Jn. 16:7). "He will glorify Me, for He will take what is mine and declare it to you" (Jn. 16:14). Hence, the glory of the cross and the shed blood is the possession of the Holy Trinity as a whole—of the Father who accepts the Son's sacrifice and glorifies Him ("all mine are thine, and thine are mine" [Jn. 17:10]), and of the Holy Spirit, who abides in the Father and thus possesses all that is the Father's, including the sacrifice and the glory of the Son. (Note by the Russian translator.)

we make the most earthly of things that give us our joy, our comfort, and our glory, or we reject what is here in favor of those things that are above, for the glory of God.

Those who seek and covet honor on this earth will have no more the power of faith in the things above to be able to seek them. Those who seek what is on the earth cannot seek what is in heaven. Those who are not truly dedicated to seeking heavenly things forfeit the glory of ascension and lose the fruits of the cross and resurrection. For Christ endured sorrows, pains, and crucifixion for the sake of the pleasure laid before Him, the pleasure of the great reconciliation in its last stage when He offered the humanity within Him to the Father, redeemed, justified, purged, and washed in blood, and seated it with Him on the right hand of the Father.

Just as the pains of the cross were crowned with resurrection, so was resurrection crowned with ascension and the sitting on the right hand of the Father. Therefore, in the ascension lies the mystery of the greatest endurance of all pain even unto death. And in sitting in the heavens with Christ there lies the utmost hope and joy and the ultimate aim of all creation old and new.

To us monks, the ascension, which represents the height of victory over the world, is our own feast, where we see ourselves soaring above the cares, the delusions, and the vanities of the world.

Consider the Lord's attitude in His ascension and all the world under His feet, and you will understand the meaning of this verse: "The Lord said to my Lord, sit at my right hand, until I make your enemies your footstool" (Ps. 110:1). Similarly, every monk who effected a genuine exodus from the world in spirit and truth, lifting his heart and mind high up in heaven, has achieved the power of ascension given to us by God in Christ now partially by the mystery, that is in mind and heart, in preparation for the entire consummation to come.

The true monk therefore lives the feast of ascension, content with the things above, in spirit and truth, all his life. He fears nothing on earth, neither tribulation, nor distress, nor persecution, nor famine, nor nakedness, nor danger, nor

sword. He covets nothing on earth, neither honor, nor friendship, nor high position, nor power, nor praise, nor name,
nor title, for he mystically feeds on the truth and love from
above; they will forget all the things of this world, forget
their people, their homeland, and even themselves.

While every person in Christ hopes for the life to come
according to the creed, the monk actually lives the world to
come because he has died to this mortal world. Ascension is
not merely our feast as monks, but it is our daily occupation
and the only life left to us.

It is very significant in the excerpt on ascension that
"while He blessed them He parted from them and was carried
up into heaven" (Lk. 24:51). We cannot enter into the state
of ascension in the spirit, or taste it, unless we are in this
very state, that is, "while we are being blessed;" we must be
in a state of prayer and blessing for everybody, for every
persecuter, everyone who offends, curses, reviles, or says all
manner of evil against us falsely. Our heart must be in a state
of total forgiveness and true peace, compassion and affection
for everyone, so we can break loose from the gravity of earth
into the sense of ascension and taste and live it in spirit and
in truth.

Again we must be in the state of "parting from them"
so that we can experience the state of being carried up above
the world by Christ. Parting from men qualifies the monk for
accepting an inner power by which he experiences a perpetual
and voluntary exodus from the world. Man ever attracts his
brother to himself seeking pride or strength or praise or
amusement, but both end up by losing themselves in this
negative attraction. Every parting from men means strength
if it is with God and in God, and will certainly prepare us
for a state of attraction to God, a spiritual ascension, truly
and mystically.

14.

Pentecost:
The Promise of the Father

The consummation of redemption

We have already dealt with the Lord's ascension forty days after His resurrection, and how He completed the redemption that He began on the cross. As He ascended on that day and crossed the barrier that separated us from the Father and entered into the inner shrine behind the curtain as a forerunner on our behalf, he entered with His blood on His hands and appeared before the Father slain in the flesh because of His love and obedience. The wrath of God for man's transgression was checked forever; the Son Himself became an offering of atonement for imperfect humanity. Hence the saying that "Jesus has gone as a forerunner on our behalf . . . thus securing an eternal redemption."

Therefore, through His ascension and His sitting at the right hand of the Father, Christ fulfilled the dispensation that came down from heaven, completing redemption and securing salvation for all who believe in Him.

After redemption

What remains after redemption and salvation is our entry into fellowship with the Father, that we may live with Him in love as children. It is one thing to die with Christ, to rise

with Him, and to sit with Him in heaven, and another to live
with the Father in the fellowship of children's love. Such
was the dispensation fulfilled by the Holy Spirit and formerly
described as the "Promise of the Father," for which the
date was fixed in the history of humankind. It was predicted
by the prophets, mentioned by Christ, and realized on Pentecost.

The revelation of love of the Father on Pentecost

We know that Christ realized the dispensation through
the flesh, namely, by death, resurrection, ascension, and sitting
at the right hand of the Father. But on Pentecost, the Father
realized the dispensation through the Holy Spirit. Whereas
the aim of Christ is salvation by the remission of sin and its
penalty and the restoration of man's relationship to God on
the basis of perpetual reconciliation, the aim of the Father is
that we should live with Him in the children's love, which
was attained on Pentecost as a result of the work of Christ.

Where the Son's role of salvation and reconciliation ended,
the Father's role of love and adoption began. Of this the
Lord expressly says: "In that day you will ask in My name;
and I do not say to you that I shall pray the Father for you;
for the Father Himself loves you, because you have loved Me
and have believed that I came from the Father" (Jn.
16:26,27).

Christ's utterance, "the Father Himself loves you" and
"in that day," was definitely fulfilled on Pentecost when the
Father sent down the Holy Spirit, His own Spirit, the Spirit
of fatherly love described as the "Promise of the Father." St.
Paul explains this in these words: "Because God's love has
been poured into our hearts through the Holy Spirit which
has been given to us" (Rm. 5:5). This means that the first
impression on our minds and hearts on this great day of
Pentecost should be the affection of the Father toward us, a
feeling of fatherly and fiery love poured out on humanity,
following the Son's fulfillment of all the requirements of
redemption and salvation.

This is our glorious share in that great day. This is the treasure of love from which the pious of all times have drawn and which has never been exhausted, the ardent fatherly love that makes us cry endlessly, "Abba! Father!" For the Spirit of Pentecost is a fiery Spirit coming fresh from the Father and conveying in its flames His compassion and His great affection that was withheld from mankind throughout thousands of years.

I wish we could realize the effectiveness and grandeur of this love, for its mystery is so profound. It has proved capable of birth, and it is like a celestial fire capable of transforming our nature just as fire transforms dust into gold. With the self-same love with which God loved His only begotten Son He chose on this "divine day"—so to speak—to love us and pour out on us His Spirit publicly. He thus turned us from slaves to children and lifted us from earth to heaven, in honor of His Son who came down to our earth and slaughtered Himself for our sake.

Adoption by the Holy Spirit

When Abraham obeyed God and was about to slay his son in submission to the voice of God Almighty, he received the bounteous grace of God who swore by himself to bless and make him a blessing. But on Pentecost, with which all our days have been blessed, when Christ had fulfilled the dispensation in the flesh, obeyed His Father even unto death on the cross, ascended and appeared before the Father in His slain body, God did something greater than an oath: His love overflowed on all humankind and He poured out on every human His Holy Spirit, where all God's grace, affection, and goodness are treasured, as Joel the Pentecost prophet predicted. With this fatherly Spirit the whole world has been blessed.

This love took the form of an adoption bond. As the Holy Father loved His Son, in the same manner and with the self-same Spirit did He love us and send "the Spirit of His Son into our hearts" (Ga. 4:6), hence, the adoption by which

we have the full right to call God "Abba! Father!" The Holy
Spirit poured out on us by the Father is itself that which
cries inside us testifying that we are the children of God.

This is the Spirit of adoption that introduced us into the
fellowship of the heritage of Christ, that is to the sonship of
God, just as St. Paul says: "But you have received the spirit of
sonship. When we cry, 'Abba! Father!' it is the Spirit Himself
bearing witness with our spirit that we are children of God,
and if children, then heirs, heirs of God and fellow heirs with
Christ" (Rm. 8:15-17).

The unction of sonship

The Father's promise of the Holy Spirit was fulfilled, and
the process of adoption long promised by the Lord and
awaited by the disciples was completed after the Son prepared
in Himself all its prerequisites and the disciples met in the
upper room according to the command, expecting the promise
and devoting themselves to prayer with one accord.

The promise was fulfilled with a fiery unction from the
Father, transmitting to us the power of an imperishable life in
communion with God, the depth of which is inexpressible
and which we now live in full manifestation. The essence of
this life is a fatherly love which in itself is life-giving, bearing the mystery of birth from above.

Christ sees His offspring, He prolongs his days; the will
of the Lord prospers in His hand; He shall see the fruit of the
travail of His soul and be satisfied (cf. Is. 53:10,11).

Great was the joy of Christ on that day when, sitting at
the right hand of the Father, He saw the Holy Spirit stamp-
ing with the Father's seal the whole dispensation which He
fulfilled with His sufferings, and when He witnessed His
disciples adopted by the Father as a Church entering upon a
new era, the era of the Father's goodwill, the era of eternal
love that was never to be taken away from it.

Christ naturally rejoiced in this because it was the petition
He had insistently offered to His Father, "that the love with
which Thou hast loved Me may be in them" (Jn. 17:26).

This is the unction of the Father that He poured out in accordance with Christ's request, and in honor of His love, upon the Church meeting with one accord on Pentecost and which still meets as a catholic Church today to receive this same unction of joy and fatherly love in the same manner as the unction of the incarnate Son on the river Jordan when He received the Spirit coming down upon Him with the Father's voice: "This is my beloved Son with whom I am well pleased" (Mt. 17:5).

This equalization between the Father's love for His Son and His love for the new man represented in the Church of the apostles meeting in the upper room surpasses all comprehension. The love poured out by the Holy Spirit from the Father onto the Son has come to be poured out also in the same manner and by the Holy Spirit from the Father on the new humanity, all those who accept redemption and adoption in Christ "that the love with which Thou hast loved Me may be in them" (Jn. 17:26).

The fellowship of love

I have already stated that the Spirit poured from the Father with the unction of love is essentially life in the Father. The Spirit here welds humankind into a communion with the Father, a communion both of love and eternal life, for the love of the Father is life, and life in communion with the Father is the ultimate love.

Christ foresaw this wonderful day, the day when the Church would live by the love of the Father, and His soul sensed comfort in the future of His little flock. So He reassured His disciples when the shadow of the cross overwhelmed them with its sorrows, "Because I live, you will live also" (Jn. 14:19). The source of this life He had already explained by saying, "I live because of the Father" (Jn. 6:57). Thus the meaning becomes clear in the combined verses: "I live because of the Father, therefore you will live with Me because of the Father."

This is the communion of life with the Father, the Son,

and the Holy Spirit that the disciples saw, lived, and enjoyed, and that, the Apostle John recorded afterwards telling us that it is the same fellowship offered now to us:

> The life was made manifest, and we saw it, and testify to it, and proclaim to you the eternal life which was with the Father and was made manifest to us—that which we have seen and heard we proclaim also to you, so that you may have fellowship with us; and our fellowship is with the Father and with His Son Jesus Christ. And we are writing this that your joy may be complete. (1 Jn. 1:2-4)

From this we gather that the fellowship with the Father obtained for us by Christ through His incarnation, when He completed it by sitting at the right hand of the Father, was the pledge, the firstfruits, the perfect pattern that, in Christ's economy, was to be the foundation for the fellowship of the life of mankind with the Father, the Son, and the Holy Spirit.

Christ's work did not end with His ascension and sitting at the right hand of glory in the highest, for it was not possible that Christ should be content, that "His joy might be complete" (1 Jn. 1:4), unless His economy were fulfilled by seeing humanity acquire a fellowship with the Father—an eternal relationship, love, and adoption equal to what He procured for us in the body of His humanity. This was the theme of a specific petition by Christ to the Father before His crucifixion: "But now I am coming to thee; and these things I speak in the world, that they may have my joy fulfilled in themselves" (Jn. 17:13).

The gifts of the Spirit have to be kindled

We can only feel this fellowship in our depths, the fellowship of love and life with the Father and the Son by the Holy Spirit which was poured out on Pentecost Day and which settled in the Church and dwelt in our temples with great meekness and humility.

It is true that the Spirit of Pentecost was tangible and visible as flames of fire. Nevertheless, this Spirit has never cooled or died down. Its fire is latent in the hearts that know how to enkindle it with prayer, humility, and love. The fire of the Holy Spirit is alive and needs only to be fanned. It awaits the oil of grace to inflame the charisms and enhance the unction. Blessed are those who gather every day even one drop of this oil, for they shall see how the Spirit burns and how the fragrant smell of Christ spreads abroad. Just as the busy bee gathers her honey from the nectar of flowers, we gather oil through vigil, self-sacrifice, and genuine meekness, through sweet poverty and joyful fasting, through ceaseless supplication, through honoring all people and giving thanks for everything, through a tongue that blesses every name.

The Holy Spirit is by nature meek and calm; His voice is never heard and His form never seen except by those that meet with one accord in the intimacy of love and await the promise of the Lord, those that open their hearts and lift their eyes to where Christ sits, demanding the right of children and seeking the face of the Father. To these the Spirit manifests Himself as a light for the inner eye and a fire that fills the heart so that every mouth overflows with the praise of God. The young shall see the "Light of the world" (Jn. 8:12) in their visions and the old realize Him in their dreams (cf. Ac. 2:16-18).

Our fellowship with the apostles

Let us not forget that through the descent of the Spirit on Pentecost, which has shone on the Church since that day and still fills us with life, light, and love, we have acquired a share with the saints enduring forever, for He is the Spirit of genuine fellowship extending from the apostles themselves without interruption since that day. We need only hold fast to this Spirit according to His promise, for He is the Spirit of the promise, holy and ever-living. We should hold Him with our hearts and never let go, breathe Him with our spirits and court Him with all affection so that we may attain our full share in Him with the saints and with Christ Himself. Just as St. Paul says: "Giving thanks to the Father, who has qualified us to share in the inheritance of the saints in light. He has delivered us from the dominion of darkness and transferred us to the Kingdom of His beloved Son" (Col. 1:12). This is the utmost wish that Christ persistently implored the Father for: "Father, I desire that they also, whom Thou hast given Me, may be with Me where I am" (Jn. 17:24).

Christ's breathing on his disciples after the resurrection and the descent of the Holy Spirit on Pentecost

Some of you have inquired about the relation of Christ's breathing of the Holy Spirit on His disciples after the resurrection to the descent of the Holy Spirit on Pentecost. About this St. Athanasius says, "Having breathed on the face of His disciples He gave them the Holy Spirit from Himself, and in this manner the Father poured it 'upon all flesh' as is written" (St. Athanasius' *Epistle on the Holy Spirit*, p. 96). That is to say that Christ gave it to the disciples, and the Father gave it to all humankind, which means that the Father completed the work of the Son on the same level or "in this manner."

I have also consulted St. Gregory the Theologian, who states:

And next in the disciples of Christ (for I omit to mention Christ Himself, in whom He dwelt, not as energizing, but as accompanying His equal), and that in three ways, as they were able to receive Him, and on three occasions; before Christ was glorified by the passion, and after He was glorified by the resurrection; and after His ascension, or restoration, or whatever we ought to call it, to heaven. Now the first of these manifests Him—the healing of the sick and casting out of evil spirits, which could not be apart from the Spirit; and so does that breathing upon them after the resurrection, which has clearly a divine inspiration; and so to the present distribution of the fiery tongues, which we are now commemorating. But the first manifested Him indistinctly, the second more expressly, this present one more perfectly, since He is no longer present only in energy, but as we may say, substantially, associating with us, and dwelling in us." ("Homily on Pentecost," *Nicene and Post-Nicene Fathers,* Vol. VII, 383.)

From the above we conclude that the work of the Holy Spirit through the breathing of Christ after the resurrection was a divine act, undefined by St. Gregory, while His descent on Pentecost was a personal existence. Here again St. Gregory did not define the nature of His work. But it seems that the relationship betwen the breathing of Christ on His disciples after the resurrection and the descent of the Spirit on Pentecost is exceedingly strong, and that the one complemented the other. The work of the Son that was fulfilled by incarnation and redemption ends at the new creation: "We have been born anew to a living hope through the resurrection of Jesus Christ from the dead" (1 Pt. 1:3). On this creation born after His image, He breathed from His Holy Spirit that in it might live, in His capacity as the creator Son and Adam the Second, the life-giving Spirit. But as the perfection of this creation had to be accomplished by the work of the Father, Christ commanded His disciples, even after this breathing, not to leave their place but to await also the "Promise of the Father," so that after they attained the "Promise of the Son" they waited to attain the "Promise of the Father." The promise of the Son is in fact a fellowship with Christ because of the Holy Spirit. Christ breathed the Holy Spirit on them after the resurrection that they might have full communion in His death and resurrection as a new creation, for without the Holy Spirit it was impossible for them to obtain a fellowship with Christ. Equally, the promise of the Father is fellowship with the Father because of the Holy Spirit through the acceptance of adoption. It is evident then that the Son's breathing on His disciples after His resurrection, and the descent of the Holy Spirit from the Father as an unction on Pentecost, both complement one action in man though they are two mystical and separate works like baptism and unction. Each of them is a sacrament of the work of the Holy Spirit (in the name of the Father, the Son, and the Holy Spirit). "He will baptize you with the Holy Spirit and with fire" (Mt. 3:11).

By baptism and unction we now receive these two acts performed by the Son (through the breathing of the Holy Spirit after His resurrection) and by the Father (through the fulfillment of His holy promise to the disciples on Pentecost) so that we can obtain what the disciples obtained after resurrection and on Pentecost, that is the new birth to a new creation, as a living Church, as the body of Christ.

The link between the gift of Pentecost and the ascension of Christ

"If I go, I will send the Counselor to you."

The Lord's saying suggests that sending the Holy Spirit on Pentecost and transmitting the unction of the Father by love and adoption in the fellowship of an eternal life with Him depended on the return of the Son to the Father, conveying in Himself the completion of His mission—a new redeemed and perfected humanity—placing it in the position of reconciliation with the Father through the honorable place which He provided us at the right hand of glory in the highest.

Having thus fulfilled His mission, meeting all the will of the Father toward us, removing all obstacles in the way of our living with the Father without blemish, Christ consequently obtained for us the promise of the Father through His sitting at His right hand as an intercessor in favor of the humanity exiled on earth. Hence the words of St. Peter on Pentecost Day: "Being therefore exalted at the right hand of God, and having received from the Father the promise of the Holy Spirit, He has poured out this which you see and hear" (Ac. 2:33).

St. Paul reveals to us the essential relationship between Christ's ascension and His sitting at the right hand of the Father, and the completion of the filling of humanity with the Holy Spirit for entry into the very fellowship completed by Christ in heaven. "He ascended far above all the heavens, that He might fill all things" (Eph. 4:10). The words "that He might" show that Christ's ascension was the beginning, the main and perpetual cause for perfecting the filling of humanity in fellowship with God. This is also elucidated by the verse, "entered as a forerunner on our behalf."

Reception of the fatherhood of God

When the hour was at hand Christ felt that humanity was in dire need of the Spirit of the Father's fatherhood so that it would no longer live an orphan without the sense of a father. Christ gratified this need, being the Son coming down from heaven, from the Father's bosom, bearing the image and compassion of the Father. Now that He was leaving them how could they survive without the care and love of God's fatherhood? He promised His disciples that on His ascension He would ask the Father to send them the Comforter, the Spirit of consolation from the Father, bringing to all humanity the affection and compassion of fatherhood as a fellowship of a life enduring forever with God the Father. Hence His words to His disciples: "I will not leave you desolate" (Jn. 14:18). The Spirit of Pentecost is in fact the Spirit of the compassion of fatherhood for comforting man that he may live as a son in the house of God forever.

On Pentecost Day the Father introduced us into a fellowship with Him which is—to some extent—of the sort existing between Him and His beloved Son. So much so that the Holy Spirit has come to transmit to us the Father's private talk with His Son, the talk of pure divine love: "When the Spirit of truth comes, He will guide you into all the truth; for He will not speak on His own authority, but whatever He hears He will speak, and He will declare to you the things that are to come. . . . He will take what is mine and declare it to you. All that the Father has is mine" (Jn. 16:13-15). Thus the Holy Spirit initiated us into the secret of the Father's fellowship with the Son. That is also what St. Paul could understand

and explain: "For the Spirit searches everything, even the depths of God," "What no eye has seen, nor ear heard, nor the heart of man conceived, what God has prepared for those who love Him, God has revealed to us through the Spirit," "Now we have received not the spirit of the world, but the Spirit which is from God, that we might understand the gifts bestowed on us by God" (1 Co. 2:9-12).

This is the Holy Spirit that the Father poured out on Pentecost in accordance with the holy promise, to acquaint us with what no heart could conceive, to initiate us into the mystery of the Father with His Son, to impart to us the fatherly love in recompense of the obedience shown by the Son toward the Father on the cross and His sufferings even unto death, and then to bestow on us all the blessings of the secrets of the fellowship between the Father and the Son.

15.

The Holy Spirit in Dogmatic Theology and in Ascetic Theology

The main thing to which we must draw attention in dealing with the dogmatic theology of St. Cyril the Great concerning the work of the Holy Spirit within the human soul—a fitting introduction to ascetic theology—is the theme that runs persistently throughout his work: πάντα ἐστὶν παρὰ Πατρὸς δι' Υἱοῦ ἐν Πνεύματι. Everything proceeds from the Father by the Son in the Holy Spirit.[1]

In other words, all that happens to the human souls is the inevitable result of the joint action of the Trinity, but the action that affects the soul directly, and which includes the whole work of the Father and the Son, is "in the Holy Spirit." The Holy Spirit does not act of His own accord, as Scripture says, "For He will not speak on His own authority, but whatever He hears He will speak" (Jn. 16:13). His entire function is to convey the work of the Father and the Son. It is the Holy Spirit who makes Christ, and all that is Christ's, whether death, resurrection, or life, our own, to be within us and to be our own possession. It is by Him too that, *through Christ,* we are made children of the Father and brought under His authority, love, guidance, and all His other gifts.

If our lives give evidence of the efficacy of the deliberate death of Christ and of His resurrection, in which He trampled on death and this world, and also the efficacy of His life,

---

[1]*In Lucam hom.* 81 (PG 72, 704); *In Ioannem* 1,5.

untainted by death, we can be certain that the Holy Spirit is active within us and that He has effectively fulfilled the will of the Son.

Likewise, if the boldness of sonship to God the Father enables us to pray fervently and uninhibitedly, inflamed by the fatherly love of God, and if our heart cries out incessantly in ardent faith and love "Abba Father," then we should understand that the Holy Spirit is present and active, that He has fulfilled the will of the Father within us.

Christ has bequeathed redemption and salvation to us by shedding His blood, but it is the Holy Spirit who executes His will and makes that redemption and salvation our own right and portion. He does not make them ours through a written document, but by sprinkling the heart with the blood of Christ, by washing the body in baptism and the sacramental act of unction. The effect of these actions is real and felt, as the heart bears witness with joy, trusting in their efficacy more than in any written document:

Let us draw near with a true heart in full assurance of faith, with our hearts sprinkled clean from an evil conscience [through the sacraments of Penance and the Eucharist] and our bodies washed with pure water. Let us hold fast the confession of our hope without wavering, for He who promised is faithful. (Heb. 10:22,23)

But beware! Let no one imagine that the Holy Spirit or His fruits can be attained by following a disciplinary program, or that they can be seen or manifested sensually, for the fruits of the Holy Spirit are exactly like His nature, invisible, audible (but no one knows where He comes from or where He goes), seen, and felt by faith alone, yet with such certainty that the witness of all five senses together could not be more sure.

However, the Holy Spirit does not stop at these sacramental actions through which He conveys to us Christ and all that belongs to Christ; we receive them simply with a heartfelt awareness. The Holy Spirit also directs His mystical activity to the mind, anointing it rationally through the Word of God, thus illuminating it. The mind becomes a partner in discerning the work of Christ that the Holy Spirit has carried out within the heart and conscience. So it is that the Holy Spirit anoints the mind and heart alike with a spiritual unction bearing the stamp, seal, and image of Christ: "In Him you also, who have heard the word of truth, the Gospel of your salvation, and have believed in Him, were sealed with the promised Holy Spirit" (Eph. 1:13).

All this means that the Holy Spirit undertakes to put us in possession of our inheritance, which is Christ and all He did for us. This takes place in the very depths of our new spiritual being, where we are branded and stamped with a living image that cannot be effaced. This is why the Holy Spirit is called "the Spirit of Christ in us" (cf. Ga. 4:6).

Likewise, the Holy Spirit brings us into our inheritance of adoption as sons making our hearts and minds actively aware of it, impressed more strongly than is the flesh by the branding iron, so that we cry out in full certitude and boldness and call upon God the Father with the lips of Christ, "Abba Father." This is why the Holy Spirit is named "the Spirit of the Father in us" (cf. Mt. 10:20), through whom we become children of God by adoption and brothers of Christ by grace.

This is what St. Cyril meant by his eloquent and profound expression, "All things are from the Father by the Son in the Holy Spirit."[2] For without the Holy Spirit the chain of contact descending from the Father to us is broken, since nothing reaches us by the Son or from the Father. Without the Holy Spirit we remain lost and wandering, away from the love of the Father and the grace of the Son, where there is no redemption, no salvation, no adoption, no confidence, no hope whatever.

When St. Cyril repeats dozens of times in his dogmatic theology that "All things are from the Father by the Son *in* the Holy Spirit," he is saying in a different way what Christ had already stressed when He said of the Holy Spirit, "For He will not speak on His own authority, but whatever He hears He will speak, and He will declare to you the things

[2]*Adversus Nestorii Blasphemias* 4, 1 (ACO 1; 1,6,77; PG 76, 172).

which are to come. He will glorify me, for He will take what
is mine and declare it to you. All that the Father has is mine;
therefore I said that He will take what is mine and declare it
to you" (Jn. 16:13-15).

Here St. Cyril emphasizes that the main concern of the
Holy Spirit for us, and His declared purpose in dwelling in
us, is totally confined to handing down and bequeathing to
us Christ and all He did, in the name, and by the will of
the Father.

This profound theological and dogmatic concept, which
the theologians recorded for the Church, was grasped by the
ascetic Fathers through their deep spiritual discernment. They
deduced from it that to acquire the Holy Spirit is to attain
the fullness of everything, for He is the Spirit of faith in
the Father and the Son, the hope of life eternal, the Spirit of
divine love and confidence before God, and the whole will
of the Father and the Son. This is why their ardent, burning
quest, their exertions, their tears, their fasting day and night
to acquire the Holy Spirit and to win His favor defy descrip-
tion and comprehension. They were certain that the spiritual
warrior strives in vain if he is not yet filled with the Holy
Spirit and is not aware of His inner action of burning, purification, and washing of the heart with the divine blood, and
of the illumination of the mind by the unction of the divine
light that it may behold the light of the glory of Christ and
the Father through the word of the Gospel. The inevitable
alternative to not being filled with the Holy Spirit is to remain
in sin, to be deprived of all the love of the Father and the
grace of the only Son.

Thus, the attributes of the Holy Spirit in ascetic theology,
which are seen through their practical application in the lives
of the Fathers, their actions and their behavior, provide the
best supporting evidence for the statement of the attributes of
the Holy Spirit found in Biblical dogmatic theology.

We also have to comprehend fully the meaning of and the
reason for the injunction of the Apostle, "Be filled with the
Spirit" (Eph. 5:18). It is an ascetic injunction based on
dogma. The commandment occurs in the imperative form,
although it is an act that surpasses the power of volition and

is beyond the scope of all human attempts or efforts to achieve. This reveals a theological mystery, that the Holy Spirit is present in the human soul prior to fullness. Since the Holy Spirit is present through baptism and chrismation, it is necessary and imperative that the Spirit who is present in us be given a chance to fill us. In other words, He should be given the freedom to work in us without hindrance until fullness is attained. Note that the verb "Be filled" as it occurs in the Greek (πληροῦσθε) is here in the imperative passive form; that is, the Spirit is the one who will fill us, if we but give Him the chance.

We always proceed from theoretical statements in dogmatic theology to practical applications in ascetic theology when we come to deal with the Holy Spirit. Dogmatic theology states theoretically that the Holy Spirit is definitely present within us through baptism and chrismation. But it remains a latent presence, inactive and unfelt by us. It is as if the Holy Spirit is idle or ineffective. This remains the case until ascetic theology intervenes by giving the commandment: "Be filled with the Spirit." We immediately find ourselves committed to inflame this gift by ascetic striving, rejecting all obstacles that would prevent the kindling of the fire of the Holy Spirit. It is then that we begin to feel the Spirit moving in our hearts.

This amazing progression from the content of theoretical theology to the effectiveness of ascetic theology might be stated as follows:

> Whereas we have unconsciously received the Holy Spirit by birth of water and the Spirit, together with chrismation, we have to live by Him in full awareness.

In other words:

> Whereas the Holy Spirit abides within us by virtue of the sacrament according to our faith and doctrine, we are commanded by God in the Gospel to be filled with the Spirit in deed. Hence, every gift from God granted us freely by faith is transformed in us into commitment

to perfect it in action. And so every grace must create
in us further grace until fullness is attained.

This in fact is the source from which ascetic theology
springs. The dogmatic belief in the Spirit is the cause, or the
deep, mystical source felt in the soul, which spurred the
Fathers on to run the race of virtue and striving toward
fullness, urging us to hasten in their steps.

Yet, however great the distance we cover along the way,
fullness of the Spirit can never induce a feeling of satisfaction,
for every fullness creates in us a new tension and a sense of
want due to the perpetual gap between the fullness we receive
in the present and that duly prepared for us in the future.
Note, too, that the greater the fullness of the Holy Spirit, the
greater the fullness of Christ. As we make room in our heart
and life for the Holy Spirit, He in turn makes room within us
for Christ. Christ is manifested in His saints to the degree to
which they can bear the fullness of the Spirit by preparing
the heart to be a comfortable home for His perpetual resi-
dence.

How precious it is, then, how indispensable, how essential
for our salvation and joy to follow the saints in their ascetic
way, meticulously examining their every piece of advice that
touches on the fullness of the Holy Spirit. Let us follow the
advice of the Apostle in full awareness, zeal, and care: "Walk
by the Spirit, and do not gratify the desires of the flesh . . .
[For] those who belong to Christ Jesus have crucified the
flesh with its passions and desires . . . If we live by the Spirit,
let us also walk by the Spirit" (Ga. 5:16,24,25). "For all
who are led by the Spirit of God are sons of God" (Rm.
8:14). We have to surrender all thought, all will, all counsel,
and all action to the Holy Spirit, that He might lead our
entire life, its past with its present and its future, using our
weakness and our strength, our success and our failure, our
health and our sickness, in pursuit of the purpose for which
"Christ died for us and was raised." "BE FILLED WITH
THE SPIRIT!"

16.

The Holy Spirit in the Conflict Between the Enemy and the Kingdom of God

The coming of the Holy Spirit on the Day of Pentecost was the beginning of the history of the Apostolic Church, for it marks the starting point of the Church's witness in the fullness of the power of the Holy Spirit. Since that day the Church has been advancing and extending under the leadership of the Holy Spirit, writing its history day by day in tears and suffering in its struggle against the spirit of this world. The Church thus follows in the steps of her bridegroom, who after He was filled with the Holy Spirit on the day of His baptism was led by the Spirit into the wilderness to be tested by Satan.

Consequently, everyone in the Church, each one who has been baptized into Christ and into the fullness of the Holy Spirit, must inevitably confront the enemy in the wilderness of this world as long as he lives, though, as with Christ, this takes place under the guidance of the Holy Spirit. This is because man's very acquisition of the Spirit of truth constitutes a declaration of war on the spirit of falsehood. "The Spirit of truth, whom the world cannot receive, because it neither sees Him nor knows Him; you know Him, for He dwells with you, and will be in you" (Jn. 14:17).

The world cannot tolerate God's chosen, the children of God, who have received the Holy Spirit and are led by Him, "for all who are led by the Spirit of God are sons of God" (Rm. 8:14).

The basic idea that inspires us in this feast, the feast of the coming of the Holy Spirit, is that if we have indeed received the Holy Spirit and loved the truth, and convenanted with Christ to keep this supreme trust, that we are sons of God, truly born from above and keeping the pledge of sonship, and we are called inescapably to this confrontation with the enemy. Christ Himself told of this at the end of His ministry, immediately before He ascended to the Father:

> If the world hates you, know that it has hated Me before it hated you. If you were of the world, the world would love its own; but because you are not of the world, but I chose you out of the world, therefore the world hates you. Remember the word that I said to you, "A servant is not greater than his master." If they persecuted Me, they will persecute you; if they kept My word, they will keep yours also. But all this they will do to you on My account . . . But when the Counselor comes, . . . the Spirit of truth, . . . He will bear witness to Me; and you also are witnesses. (Jn. 15:18-27)

So it is that Christ's temptation by the devil in the wilderness after He was anointed and filled with the Holy Spirit took place for us as we confront the spirt of this world. It is our only guiding principle as we stand against the enemy on our journey through life, whether we consider the struggle of the Church as a whole or the struggle of each individual who has been baptized into Christ and has received the unction of the Holy Spirit in the Church. This is to say that we do not face any temptation alone; Christ did not receive the unction primarily for Himself, but was anointed by the Holy Spirit that we might be filled and underwent temptation in order that His victory might become our first victory over the power of evil and darkness that held sway over Adam.

It is not for nothing that Christ, after emerging victorious from all the temptations of Satan, "was with the wild beasts;

and the angels ministered to Him" (Mk. 1:13; Mt. 4:11). Here Adam returns to his condition before the fall. Christ has regained what Adam lost. Immediately after being driven out from the presence of God because of his transgression, Adam lost his friendship with and supremacy over the beasts and his harmony with the heavenly creation. This is why man's companionship with animals, along with his seeing the angels, became after the fall of Adam one of the dreams of the Messianic age. In prophecy it is regarded as a prominent feature of the restoration of God's good will toward humanity. "The wolf shall dwell with the lamb, and the leopard shall lie down with the kid, and the calf and the lion and the fatling together, and a little child shall lead them" (Is. 11:6). Note here that the "little child" represents the childhood that is the return of man to the Kingdom of God" (Mt. 18:3). It is also a veiled and amazingly profound reference to the new birth received in baptism. "Like newborn babes, long for the pure spiritual milk, that by it you may grow up" (1 Pt. 2:2).

Christ here fulfilled the Messianic dream and led man into the Kingdom of God in deed and in power. "If it is by the finger of God that I cast out demons, then the Kingdom of God has come upon you" (Lk. 11:20). As Clement of Alexandria says, "The angels came and served Him as true King of creation" (Exc. Theod. 85).

Christ, by being anointed and filled with the Holy Spirit in the Jordan, and by His victory over Satan, restored to humanity its authority over the devil and the power of evil, and set it once more at harmony with the beasts of the earth and the whole creation. He also reconciled humanity with the angels who instead of being set, wielding flaming swords, to prevent man from returning to Paradise, became once more spirits sent to minister to those of the sons of Adam who were ready to inherit salvation.

To those who believe in Him, Christ gave this same active power, that is, the unction of the Holy Spirit and the fullness of His gifts and power, so that whoever believes in His name could attain the same victory over the attacks of the enemy and the same reconciliation with the heavenly creatures not only for salvation but also to serve salvation.

This is why we find that divinely inspired Scripture makes no distinction between what the Messiah will accomplish in His person on our behalf, and what will be attributed to us because of Him and by the power of His name and Spirit. The Spirit refers to this same victory in the Psalms, where we find that the "righteous" man is victorious over the powers of evil.

> He who dwells in the shelter of the Most High . . . [and] finds refuge under His wings; His faithfulness is a shield and buckler. [He] fears not the terror of the night, nor the arrow that flies by day, nor the pestilence that stalks in darkness, nor the destruction that wastes at noonday. A thousand may fall at your side, ten thousand at your right hand; but it will not come near you. You will only look with your eyes and see the recompense of the wicked. Because you have made the Lord your refuge, the Most High your habitation, no evil shall befall you, no scourge come near your tent. For He will give His angels charge of you to guard you in all your ways. On their hands they will bear you up, lest you dash your foot against a stone. You will tread on the lion and the adder [i.e. the devil and the powers of evil], the young lion and the serpent you will trample under foot. Because He cleaves to me in love, I will deliver Him; I will protect Him, because He knows my name. When He calls to me, I will answer Him; I will be with Him in trouble, I will rescue Him and honor Him. With long life I will satisfy Him, and show Him my salvation. (Ps. 91)

This Psalm describes the victory of the Messiah, who dwells on high. It paints a detailed picture of His temptation in the wilderness and His battle with the devil, and then tells of the submission of the beasts and the ministrations of the angels. Then it goes on, without referring to any break in time or change of persons, to speak of the victory of those who will dwell under His protection and cleave to His name. This is one of the most powerful of the Psalms because of its ability to strengthen the heart of the Christian in his invisible warfare with the powers of the enemy; it gives a pledge of victory that is still effective, since Christ fulfilled all its requirements in the wilderness and Gethsemane and on Golgotha and by the Holy Spirit imparted His victory to all who cleave to the name of the Lord when they undergo temptation.[1]

When we examine this inevitable conflict with the enemy and study its causes and aims, we find, amazingly, that it is the Holy Spirit who is the instigator of the war with the powers of evil and darkness, and that it is He too who is the guarantor of victory and the effective power that can never be overcome. As soon as Christ was anointed and filled with the Holy Spirit, who is against this world, He was led out by the Holy Spirit Himself to be tempted by Satan. So it is also with us; as soon as we receive the Holy Spirit and are baptized and anointed and enlightened and filled with the Spirit of truth, it is as if we have declared war on the devil, and we

---

[1]The Psalmody (sung to the vatos tune) to the Lord Jesus with the Theotokia of Friday contains the following lines:

I have submitted myself to a great principle,
the saving name of our Lord Jesus Christ.
Our Lord Jesus Christ gave a sign to His servants who fear Him,
that they might flee from the bow.
Our Lord Jesus Christ gave a sign to His servants who fear Him,
that they might stop the mouths of lions.
Our Lord Jesus Christ gave a sign to His servants who fear Him,
that they might put out fire.
Our Lord Jesus Christ gave a sign to His servants who fear Him,
that they might cast out devils.
Our Lord Jesus Christ gave a sign to His servants who fear Him,
that they might vanquish their enemies.
The sign is the saving name of our Lord Jesus Christ
and the life-giving Cross on which He was crucified.
Blessed is the man who has no concern for this life
and its soul-destroying affairs,
Who takes up his cross day by day and cleaves with his heart
and mind to the saving name of our Lord Jesus Christ.
Our heart rejoices and our tongue is filled with praise
when we repeat the saving name of our Lord Jesus Christ.
Whenever we sing, let us sweetly say,
"Lord Jesus Christ have mercy on our souls."

immediately enter into the struggle with the powers of darkness and the spirit of falsehood, which holds sway over the
thinking of this world and forces it into evil and sin.

All this should illumine our understanding so that we
revise our evaluation of the meaning of temptation in general,
and of the causes and sources of the attacks the world makes
upon us that the devil skillfully aims in our direction. We
should never consider this subject on a purely individual level,
for even though temptations arise according to the stature of
each believer and are limited by God so that they do not
surpass the ability of each person to endure, according to his
faith and steadfastness, temptations in general are nevertheless an inevitable product of the interaction between the Spirit
of God, who is leading us into His Kingdom, and the powers
of evil and darkness, which stand between us and our high
calling. Now Christ does not leave us to struggle along the
ways in our own feeble power, for He opened up the way to
victory for us when He overcame the prince of this world, the
source of evil, saying, "Be of good cheer, I have overcome the
world" (Jn. 16:33) and, "The ruler of this world is coming.
He has no power over me" (Jn. 14:30). He has given us
power to overcome, in His name, all the powers of darkness
and all the works of evil, so long as we cleave to His name
and the Holy Spirit. "And such were some of you [under the
power of fornication, theft, greed, drunkenness, and vilifica-
tion]. But you were washed [i.e. baptized], you were sancti-
fied [by the blood, therefore, the holy things to those who
are holy"], you were justified in the name of the Lord Jesus
Christ and in the Spirit of our God" (1 Co. 6:11). Here
the name of Christ and the Holy Spirit remind us once again
of the person of Christ, coming up out of the Jordan filled with
the Holy Spirit and making His way out into the wilderness
to face the great temptation and take on the powers of darkness.

We should note well that the devil does not make war
using methods that are obvious to the ordinary mind or
accessible to human logic and intelligence.

²From the Coptic liturgy.

The mystery of lawlessness is already at work [i.e. hidden actions are all deception and deceit]; only He who now restrains it will do so until he is out of the way. And then the lawless one will be revealed, and the Lord Jesus will slay him with the breath of His mouth [the Holy Spirit] and destroy him by His appearing and His coming. The coming of the lawless one by the activity of Satan will be with all power and with pretended signs and wonders, and with all wicked deception for those who are to perish, because they refused to love the truth and so be saved. Therefore God sends upon them a strong delusion, to make them believe what is false, so that all may be condemned who did not believe the truth but had pleasure in unrighteousness. (2 Th. 2:7-12)

Because of this hidden deceit and the fraudulent methods the devil uses, all who do not cleave to the name of Christ and the Holy Spirit—that is, the Spirit of truth, knowledge, understanding, and divine guidance—easily fall prey to the devil's wiles and do his works quite unaware. Instead of rightly perceiving the works of the evil one, they see them simply as the way of the world or the prevailing custom or the natural product of human nature or perhaps the result of sickness, chance, unintentional error, or rash speech or action. These are the threads the devil cleverly weaves together till they invisibly encircle the mind, gradually and fiendishly shutting out the light that brings discernment between truth and falsehood. Then they close in upon the conscience, stifling it till it slowly and almost imperceptibly loses its sensitivity to truth. Finally these perceptions penetrate so deeply that they enslave not only the mind, but even the body itself, and in the end the law of sin occupies a person's very being and controls mind, tongue, conscience, body, and behavior.

It is the Holy Spirit, the Spirit of truth, the Spirit of wisdom and right guidance, who alone can reveal in power and righteousness the movements and sly tricks of the devil in his thinking, conscience, behavior, and his body itself, no matter how deceptive they may be. The Holy Spirit has a greater, deeper, and wider power than the deception of the devil, and He brings it to bear when we throw ourselves down beneath the cross and ask for help. The Spirit of truth is immeasurably stronger than the spirit of evil and reveals all the tricks of the devil, firmly overcoming them one by one and giving illumination, understanding, and irresistible divine wisdom. As the Apostle Paul says, "We are not ignorant of his designs" (2 Co. 2:11).

In our warfare we must have a clear understanding that the work of the Holy Spirit for God's chosen is to aid those who are tempted. He is not instructed to do so, nor does He need to be entreated; this is His special work. Any temptation that attacks one who has received the Holy Spirit and believed in Christ is counted by the Spirit as a temptation directed at Christ Himself, who is truth; it is a temptation directed at God. In this situation the Holy Spirit carries out a divine work according to His own good pleasure; it is His own special function springing from His own nature. This is why the Apostle Paul stresses that God is faithful in what concerns Him; that is to say He is faithful to the truth. He does not, therefore, allow anyone to be tempted by evil or falsehood beyond his capacity to resist, but provides a way of escape from human temptation. This way of escape is through the speedy, sure, and faithful intervention of the Holy Spirit to lift man up above his own level and minister to those who are tempted, maintaining the validity of the temptation of Christ, and so vindicating truth against falsehood and gaining a victory for Christ, who paid the price of victory over the world on behalf of every believer. The Holy Spirit, when He supports us in temptation, bears witness to Christ within us, and helps us to bear witness to Christ too. "[The Holy Spirit] bears witness to me, and you also are witnesses" (Jn. 15:26,27).

So we see that it is the Holy Spirit who alerts us and reveals the evil that lies in wait for us, the works of falsehood, and the malice of the devil that we encounter in the war between light and darkness within human nature. If only we had complete confidence that, just as the devil only makes war on the believers who are filled with the Holy Spirit, so also the Holy Spirit could not possibly abandon believers in Christ who have each been led to the Holy Spirit and loved Him, clinging to Him and acquiring Him as truth and life. "The Lord knows how to rescue the godly from trial, and to keep the unrighteous under punishment until the day of judgment" (2 Pt. 2:9). It is true that the devil is able to make us blind through sin and by our following after evil and the doers of evil, and is also able to introduce into our nature ignorance, forgetfulness, absent-mindedness, sloth, carelessness, and apathy, using all these as effective weapons to bind his prey and make us obedient instruments. But we find that the Holy Spirit, to counteract all of this, grants to the renewed nature of those in whom He dwells:

Illumination: "That you may declare the wonderful deeds of Him who called you out of darkness into His marvelous light" (1 Pt. 2:9).

Understanding: "I bless the Lord who gives me counsel" (Ps. 16:7), for the Holy Spirit is the Spirit of guidance and understanding.

Knowledge of the principles of truth: This is one of the essential attributes of the nature of the Holy Spirit and it is acquired by those who cleave to the Lord: "The Spirit of truth who teaches you all things" (Jn. 16:13). "The Lord God has given me the tongue of those who are taught, that I may know how to sustain with a word him that is weary" (Is. 50:4).

Inner alertness of the heart: "Morning by morning He wakens, He wakens my ear to hear as those who are taught. The Lord God has opened my ear, and I was not rebellious, I turned not backward" (Is. 50:4,5).

These are the attributes of the new nature of the new man born of water and the Spirit. The Holy Spirit grants them to all who believe in Christ and are baptized, bearing witness to truth against falsehood and all the powers of evil, so that they may live by them in perfect enlightenment, understanding, knowledge, and alertness, perceiving not only evil itself, but all that resembles evil. When these qualities exist in us, they are the practical evidence of the indwelling of the Holy Spirit.

Our Lord pointed out this truth, quoting the prophets: "It is written in the prophets, 'And they shall all be taught by God' " (Jn. 6:45). "If any man's will is to do His [God's] will, he shall know whether the teaching is from God or whether I am speaking on my own authority" (Jn 7:17).

We might almost say that perception, enlightened by the Holy Spirit and committed to divine truth, is the strongest weapon that can be used to defeat the devil when he is at work in the mind of man, trying to corrupt the conscience to allow the follies of sin and evil. The devil can only enter us through our mind and imagination, for sin begins with a movement of the mind and can only be ended by enlightenment that reveals how false falsehood is. We can only acquire this mental enlightenment by the Holy Spirit, or by the word of God (Scripture), for the word is at one and the same time a work of the Holy Spirit, the power of God bearing divine authority, and the essential mind that forms and builds all minds. This is why the Lord uses Scripture, a terrifying weapon against the deceit of the devil: "It is written, 'You shall not tempt the Lord your God' " (Mt. 4:7). Neither must we ever forget that the word of Christ is itself spirit and life, or that the whole Bible is inspired by God, written through the Holy Spirit. It is for this reason that the "word" found in the Gospel is an effective means of directly and constantly drawing near to the Spirit and mind of God for anyone who believes in Christ, for it bestows mental illumination, and even the power and authority of God, that reveals and brings to nothing all the maneuvers of the devil. The result of this is victory over the world and a greater share in the mystery of eternal life.

Just as Christ cast out devils by the Spirit of God and became an object of terror to the devil and his hosts, so too His name and His word (Spirit and life) became terrifying, for His word bears the same authority as His person. Christ showed this clearly when He gave His disciples authority to cast out devils. "And He called to Him His twelve disciples and gave them authority [the authority of the Holy Spirit] over unclean spirits, to cast them out" (Mt. 10:1). Christ's authority, which He gave to His disciples with the order to "cast out devils," was contained in a prayer in His name. "Lord, even the demons are subject to us in your name" (Lk. 10:17). This very authority was transferred at Christ's command from the disciples to the Church, that is, to the believers, forever: "And these signs will accompany those who believe: in My name they will cast out demons" (Mk. 16:17).

The Apostle Paul therefore considered that devotion to the name of Christ, together with adherence to the Holy Spirit, was the source of cleansing from the stain of sin and the source of sanctification in God and justification of all condemnation unto salvation. Paul also considered that the "word," since it is invested with the power of the Holy Spirit who inspired it, is by itself able to make a person wise unto salvation. "From childhood you have been acquainted with the sacred writings which are able to insruct you for salvation through faith in Jesus Christ. All Scripture is inspired by God" (2 Tm. 3:15,16).

When the Bible speaks of casting out demons in the name of Christ, itself a phenomenon that has accompanied believers through the ages, its intention is to reveal the extent of the authority and supremacy that have become ours, by the name of Christ and the Holy Spirit, and to uncover the works of the devil and observe his actions and designs in the mind and heart of man. It reveals, too, the capability we have for bringing them all to nothing, for the believer has received authority from God and in the name of Christ to cast out the devil himself and destroy his habitation in the body of another human being. So it is not difficult for him to thwart his designs and reject his ideas and plans from his own soul, destroying his workings of the conscience and his law that waits in ambush in his body. But this can only come into effect through the Holy Spirit, who dwells in the heart, as we have said, so that the individual is trained in how to arrive humbly and simply at the counsel of the Holy Spirit, the Counselor.

The Bible distinguishes between the power to cast out the devil (which Christ gave to the disciples and then to the

believers in general, and which appeared most clearly and
supremely in casting out the devil from people's bodies and
in his open expulsion from the dwelling he had made in
them) and the lesser power, as the Apostle Paul sees it, of
overcoming his deception and cunning by squashing the
insinuations of the devil and all pride that rises up against
the knowledge of God, and by bringing every thought into
the capitivity of obedience to Christ in the sure knowledge
that our warfare is with the devil. Even though it takes place
in the body, this warfare is not fought with actual weapons
but with the power of God, that is, the Holy Spirit (cf. 2
Co. 10:3-6).

Here we must consider carefully what is Christ's aim in
giving us authority over the devil, whether it be by casting
him out or by overcoming his wickedness and his instigations.
It is not an authority simply to grant us supremacy or mastery
so we can grow in self-confidence or rejoice in our victories.
The seventy disciples made that mistake once when they
returned in jubilation. "The seventy returned with joy, saying,
'Lord, even the demons are subject to us in your name.' " And
He said to them, warning them and correcting them, "Do
not rejoice in this, that the spirits are subject to you; but
rejoice that your names are written in heaven" (Lk. 10:17,20).
Here it is clear that the authority Christ gives us through
His name, over the devil and the powers of evil so we can
bring them into submission, is basically a sign of our being
chosen and adopted. Our names are written for our salvation
in heaven with the chosen and not simply so that we should
exercise mastery over the devil.

Christ defeated the devil for us so that we would not be
defeated by him, and for this reason our names are written
in heaven. Christ was victorious because He is the Son of
God, and we because He granted us victory, for we have
become sons of God in Him. Victory over the devil is therefore first and foremost a sign that we are chosen and adopted
in Christ and through Christ. He did not give us authority
to trample on every power of the enemy simply so we would
rejoice and boast of our power; it was rather so we would
not fear the enemy and be defeated by his deceptions and

falsehoods, because then he would deprive us of the mastery and victory that are ours in Christ and deprive us of our salvation and everlasting life as His chosen.

To put it more clearly and concisely, we may say that we have been given the power to defeat the kingdom of the devil so that the Kingdom of God might rule supreme and the power to cast out the devil so the Holy Spirit may dwell in us and trample on every power of the enemy so that the power of the Holy Spirit may control our whole life. It is also the power to bring to nothing all the tricks and ideas and plans of the devil so we can acquire the mind and holiness of Christ. This is the work of Christ and the Holy Spirit against the devil and all the power of the enemy in our lives, and this is how the Kingdom of God is founded on striving, sweat, and tears and through constant, relentless struggle.

Look at Christ in Gethsemane in the final stages of the crucial battle against the devil. This fearsome sight, of Christ on His knees beseeching the Father three time while His sweat fell to the ground in painful drops like blood, shows us what it means to confront and challenge the enemy in our life and reveals the meaning of the struggle against the powers of darkness ("This is your hour, and the power of darkness" [Lk. 22:53]) by praying through the night. It also shows the meaning of standing firm and confronting the temptor even to the shedding of blood in the most decisive stage of the conflict that ended with the cross. This short time that Christ spent alone in His unseen battle with the devil and his forces before the cross was equivalent in violence, by Christ's own reckoning, to a war undertaken by more than twelve armies of angels: "Do you think that I cannot appeal to my Father, and He will at once send me more than twelve legions of angels?" (Mt. 26:53).

Christ, knowing the extent of the suffering we would undergo after His ascension when we faced the powers of darkness and the ruler of this world with all his evil ones and wickedness, gave us assurance that He would not leave us desolate in this war. It would not be at all an equal struggle if we entered into it alone: "While I was with them [in the world], I kept them in Thy name . . . But now I am coming

to Thee . . . The world has hated them because they are not
of the world, even as I am not of the world . . ." (Jn.
17:12-14). Christ describes the depth of the struggle that
has been bequeathed to us to undertake against the powers
of darkness in the world for the sake of the name of Christ
after His ascension. This is why He sent the Holy Spirit, the
Comforter. "I will pray the Father, and He will give you
another Counselor, to be with you forever, even the Spirit of
truth . . . I will not leave you desolate; I will come to you . . .
You [are] in me and I in you . . . The Counselor, the Holy
Spirit, whom the Father will send in My name, He will teach
you all things, and bring to your remembrance all that I have
said to you" (Jn. 14:16-26).

With these words Christ gave a full guarantee of the
victory of all those who strive for His Kingdom, by sending
the Holy Spirit to give comfort, by teaching, and through
knowledge of the truth and recollection of the words of the
Lord as a basis for strength and combat and as essential
weapons in our long war against the spirit of evil in the
world.

And so from the day of Pentecost until now, the Holy
Spirit has interceded for us in our warfare and strife, in our
sadness and suffering, with groanings that cannot be uttered.

17.

The Assumption of the Body of the Virgin Mary[1]

This day is an occasion for honoring the body of the Virgin. The assumption of her body is a supreme act of reverence on the part of heaven. The Orthodox doctrine of honoring the bodies of saints does not stem from a vacuum. After a lengthy interview with God in which Moses received the commandments and the Law, his face radiated with a light the Israelites could not bear to look at. The light that his face reflected was a divine light, and divine light expresses divine presence. God was visible in the face of Moses, therefore the reprobate people refrained from looking at his face because sin and God cannot meet face to face. Hence the veil that Moses wore and that St. Paul regarded as a symbol of spiritual blindness.

St. Paul went on to say that if ministering to the Law that brought about condemnation and death created such glory visible to the flesh and such shining to the human face, much more the glory that is created by ministering to righteousness!

On this ground we base our view concerning the Virgin, her body, and her face. If the face of Moses shone when he received mere words written by the finger of God, expressing the glory which came over the body, how much more was the glory which came over the body of the Virgin when she

[1]The feast of the Assumption of the Body of Virgin Mary is celebrated in the Coptic Church on the 22nd of August.

received in her womb the very Word of God, the Son of God Himself, who assumed a body from her body after preparation by the Holy Spirit and a total overshadowing by the power of God from inside and outside! What glory then came over the body of the Virgin!

We all know how God ended Moses' life and buried him in Mount Nebo far from the people's sight lest they should err and worship his body, for it seems that it radiated even after death. Hence it was said of him in the book of Deuteronomy: "No man knows the place of his burial to this day." Again we have a special mention of the body of Moses in the Epistle of Jude. When the Archangel Michael, contending with the devil, disputed about the body of Moses he said to him, "The Lord rebuke you." This suggests that the Archangel Michael had been charged with guarding this body or carrying it up to heaven, and when the devil tried to restore it or reveal its burial place in order to mislead the people, a battle broke out between them and the Archangel invoked the aid of the Lord as the head of the heavenly host.

If God had taken such care to undertake personally the burial of Moses and to assign to the Archangel Michael the task of guarding the body or perhaps carrying it up into heaven—in accordance with the Jewish tradition—and all this because the body of Moses reflected the light and glory of God on account of his presence before God for forty days and his receipt of written commandments, then honoring bodies in Orthodox doctrine does not stem from a vacuum. How much greater care was given by God and Christ Himself to the body of the Virgin after her death, the body which obtained a permanent descent of the Holy Spirit, a fullness of grace, a special overshadowing by the power of the Most High, and finally the dwelling of the Word of God for nine months in her womb! It is true that we have no report that the body of the Virgin shone with heavenly light, but this we know for sure was a further extension of the process of divesting as experienced by Christ to conceal the glory of His divinity. Even the body of Christ Himself throughout His life did not shine except once and for a brief period on the day of the transfiguration, although He is the true light of the world, ever-shining for everyone.

It is evident then that there was a divine plan to conceal all the glory of Christ, and consequently of the Virgin, lest belief in Christ should surpass its designed limits, lest the cross should lose its disgrace and the veneration of the Virgin should slip into a cult or apotheosis exclusively appropriated by God.

Just like the death of Moses, that of the Virgin had to take place quietly, especially since at the time of her death the Gospel was broadly proclaimed and Christ was known to be the true Son of God born of the Virgin Mary. This is why there is no mention of the Virgin's death in the Gospels or the Epistles. Consequently the assumption of her body was transmitted only through secret tradition during the first three centuries, so she would not come too much into the lime-light and so the worship of God would not deviate from its proper course.

If the body of Moses, because it shone with the light of God, required God to undertake its burial and charge the Archangel Michael with guarding it, then there is no cause for wonder if we hear that Christ Himself came at the death of the Virgin, received her holy spirit, and carried it up to heaven. As for her body, it was undoubtedly left in charge of the Archangel Michael[2] until it was lifted to heaven at the fixed time. So the body of the Virgin, which was the subject of care by the divine Father since the moment of annunciation and the receipt of the divine conception, continued to be honored until God lifted it with angelic reverence.

Our honoring the body of the Virgin is part and parcel of our belief in eschatological things—things relating to the life to come—for it is well known that the resurrection of bodies is essential to Christ's work in the hereafter. Though the assumption of the Virgin's body is not really an act of resur-rection, it is a state of transfiguration in which the body was carried on the hand of angelic powers in preparation for a resurrection fulfilled or to be fulfilled there.

[2]Archangel Gabriel, according to the Greek Orthodox tradition. [Note by a Russian translator].

The New Testament abounds with instances of transfiguration. Christ began this eschatological act in Himself, in the
flesh that He took from us, on the mount of transfiguration
with Peter, John, and James, making it shine more brigthly
than the sun, being the firstfruit and the prototype of our
bodies when their redemption would be complete. Since then,
humankind, even the whole creation, has been groaning in
travail together and until now has been waiting for the
adoption as sons, the redemption of our bodies. The whole
creation, and not only our bodies, is invited to this transfiguration. The fact that the garments of Christ became glistening,
more white than snow, clearly indicates that Christ is the light
of the world and of creation, and that all creatures will
assume their new form from the coming Christ.

Honoring the holy and luminous bodies is an eschatological act, an extension of the transfiguration across the
present age, a life of faith preparatory for the life to come.
Since the transfiguration day, Christ has not ceased to pour
out His light on the bodies and faces of His saints. The
wilderness of Scete is witness to this fact, and has won an
abundant share in receiving the celestial light. Seven eminent
fathers testified that they had seen St. Macarius the Great
shining in the darkness inside his cell. In the death hour of
St. Sesoes, the fathers who were sitting around him witnessed
his face radiating with a light that gradually increased until
he gave up the spirit. Then the light became as dazzling as
lightning and the cell was filled with the odor of incense. It
was also reported that God so honored Abba Pambo that it
was hard for anyone to gaze at his face because of the glory
that shone from him, he looked so much like a king on his
throne. When the disciples of St. Arsenius entered his cell
suddenly while he was praying they found his whole body
alight like fire. St. Joseph the Great was seen praying; he
was lifting up his hands and his fingers looked like ten flames
of fire.

In these and other instances of luminous faces and bodies
we can only see a true extension of the transfiguration of
Christ across Pentecost in the descent of the Holy Spirit like
tongues of fire resting on the bodies and preparing them for

the transfiguration and resurrection to come. Honoring saints' bodies in Orthodox doctrine is in fact a continuation of St. Peter's joy at the radiating light of Christ, and of his impulsive words of faith: "Master, it is well that we are here."

The transfigured Lord is present in His saints, and His light and Holy Spirit shine in their bodies and spirits. Sanctification sometimes goes beyond the spirit and the soul to affect and fill the body. Though the body exists in the world it is reckoned not of this world, but on earthly and heavenly bread together and is illuminated by the light of this world and of heaven together. Is not that a response to the Apostle's call, "Glorify the Lord in your bodies"?

Today's commemoration of the assumption of the Virgin's body is truly a glorification of the Lord who continues to be glorified every day in His saints: "So that the name of our Lord Jesus may be glorified in you, and you in Him" (2 Th. 1:12).

18.

The Virgin in the Theology of the Church

The Virgin and the human race

"Behold, I am the handmaid of the Lord; let it be to me according to your word" (Lk. 1:38).

These first recorded words of the Virgin reveal awesome depths of her character, but unfortunately because we tend to concentrate on her youth and simplicity, we pass over her words without pondering over them and so miss their depth.

The Virgin here is taking a firm and decisive stand with respect to herself, the world, and God. She believed the annunciation of the angel and perceived that it was a heavenly proclamation that she had indeed been chosen to bear in her womb a child begotten by God without human seed. God would be His father directly, so He would be called Holy, one of the most special and supreme attributes of God. He would also be called Son of the Most High, and Emmanuel (God is with us). When Mary believed this she gave herself to God as His handmaid, or slave, in the sense that she committed herself totally to Him, body, soul, and spirit. By this commitment, which took the form almost of an oath or everlasting covenant, the Virgin consecrated her whole life to God after the mystery had taken place in her. According to this covenant that she took upon herself, she became, as far as she herself was concerned, committed to virginity, and as far as the world was concerned, she became the supreme example of purity, and as far as God was concerned, she became a slave, completely owned by Him and living for Him alone. Her heart, which God made his possession through the Holy Spirit, beat now only for the sake of the holy Word of God that was born of her.

We cannot overlook the feelings and emotions that were shared by the Virgin Mother and the Holy One who was born her son. The Virgin gave all her love and affection as a mother to the Christ she bore, and Christ reciprocated as her son with the same emotions and affection, showing her obedience, as the Gospel says. It is true that she was a handmaid, but the handmaid of God became the mother of the Son of God, though by her vow of total submission and obedience, the mother remained a handmaid.[1]

When the Virgin understood clearly through the annunciation that she was to become the mother of the Holy One, the Son of God, she vowed that she would be a handmaid of God all her life. How different from Adam and Eve, who refused the word of God and deliberately and willfully ate of the food that God had forbidden them, intending to become like God Himself. The Virgin, by her words of commitment—"Behold, the handmaid of the Lord; be it unto me according to Thy word"—took Adam and Eve back to their state before the fall. Adam and Eve rejected the living and life-giving word of God and so the sentence of death was passed on them. The Virgin accepted the Word of God, the Word of life, and He entered into her and removed from her the curse of death: "Blessed are you among women" (Lk. 1:42). The Virgin's words, "Behold, the handmaid of the Lord," which come after God had elevated her to be the mother of His Son, the Holy One, reveal her determination to go back before the fall and openly repudiate the sin of Adam and Eve.

[1]The Church weaves these two contrasting titles into a hymn that fills man with a sense of the greatness of the joy and hope the Virgin brought to a humanity living in servitude. "Rejoice, Mary, handmaid and mother, for the angels worship Him whom you hold upon your lap" (Troparion to the Virgin in the Coptic Liturgy). The Virgin, and with her the whole human race, is here elevated through the glory of motherhood, for she transformed our servitude into a way for us to receive and bear the Word of God in us.

The Virgin is here a fine model of the person to whom the Holy Spirit has granted the indwelling of the Word of God. That person is able to return through humility to eternal life, to the state of man before the fall. The promise that the Word of God would enter into the womb of the Virgin through His amazing self-denial, by which the incarnation was accomplished, was fulfilled through the mystery of the Virgin's wondrous humility. And it will always be through our humility alone that we shall mysteriously be fitted to partake of union with God.

The Apostle Paul, when he received the fullness of the Holy Spirit, followed the same path as the Virgin. After receiving the freedom of the sons of God, after God in His mercy revealed to him mysteries that had been hidden through the ages and were revealed only to the Apostles, after he was raised up through many revelations to see the heavens in all their glory, and after he saw Jesus Himself and received perfect freedom from Him—"Am I not free? . . . Have I not seen Jesus our Lord" (1 Co. 9:1)—after all this he deliberately declared that he was Paul, "a servant of Jesus Christ" (Rm. 1:1). Servitude to God is our joyful gift to God, for those who enter into the freedom of the children of God cannot but offer that freedom back to God once more as a sacrifice of love and become the slave of the supreme tender love of the Father.

Servitude here is the servitude of love for God and it is a fruit of freedom. No one can serve God freely in fullness of spirit, heart, and mind unless he has been freed of the corruption that is characteristic of this world and of the passions and pride of the self, by the effective, purifying indwelling of the Word of God in the depths of his mind and heart.

The Virgin is above the prophets

In the theology of the Church the Virgin remains very near to God, and therefore her holiness and efficacy as inter-

cessor are greater than those of the prophets, for the mystery
of the Virgin is greater than the gift of prophecy.

The prophets were inspired by the Holy Spirit in their
minds and speech to declare the word of God at a set time
in history. The Virgin, on the other hand, received the Holy
Spirit in such a way that He was united with her whole being,
so that the Word of God could take from her flesh and blood
a body for Himself. Moreover, the word of God that was
spoken by the prophets was a word in time intended to teach,
and it was adaptable, changing from generation to generation,
while the Word of God who came forth from the Virgin's
womb was the person of the eternal Son of God, the life-
giving Word who speaks to us in love and life till the end
of time.

The Virgin's gift to us of "the Word of God" was different from that of the prophets, and the relationship that was
formed and endured between her and the Word of God was
unique. The prophets were vessels who bore the divine word
for a time, but then it left them and they became once again
strangers to the word of life. But the Virgin was bound to
the Word of God as His mother, just as He was bound to
her as her Son, and she is eternally the mother of the Son
of God in so far as the Son of God continues to be the Son
of Man.

The Virgin as prophetess

Evidence for the correctness of the Church's doctrine that
the Virgin is above the prophets lies in the fact that the
Virgin herself prophesied and gave a prophecy greater than
that of the prophets. Is this really true?

Logically it was impossible for the Virgin to conceive the
Word of God and not prophesy. And indeed as soon as the
living Word of God the Father took up His dwelling in the
Virgin's womb, she was filled with the joy of salvation and
opened her mouth praising the name of God the Holy One
and speaking of the wonders of God. "And Mary said, 'My
soul magnifies the Lord, and my spirit rejoices in God my

Savior, for He has regarded the low estate of His hand-maiden. For behold, henceforth all generations will call me blessed; for He who is mighty has done great things for me, and holy is His name' " (Lk. 1:46-49).

This is the song of praise of a prophetess who has received a supreme prophetic revelation extending in time to all generations. If we examine the prophecy we find that it has indeed been fulfilled throughout the past two thousand years. The phrase, "henceforth all generations will call me blessed," is one of the most significant of those spoken by the Virgin; it is unheard of for a prophet to say, "Henceforth all generations will call me blessed; for He who is mighty has done great things for me." On the contrary, we hear Isaiah the prophet saying, "Woe is me, for I am lost, for I am a man of unclean lips" (Is. 6:5). The Virgin, with these amazing words, reveals clearly the relationship and closeness to God that she experienced beyond the rest of humankind. She proclaims at once boldly and humbly that mighty God has granted her a position of permanent honor on earth and in heaven, after her departure from this life.

It is true that anyone can be honored by God for some action he has performed, but that it should be granted to any individual that he be honored by all generations, that is by the whole human race throughout the ages forever, not as a reward for a particular action or in recognition of deeds performed, but because of a worthiness bestowed by God through great things He did for that person—this is completely unheard of in the whole of human history.

We therefore stand before a great prophecy which sheds light on the person of the Virgin and sets her on a level higher than all other prophets and human beings. Her blessedness is a state higher than that of humankind, for she receives it from God through her humility and worthiness to bear the Word of God. But what is striking is that her being called blessed by all generations appears here to unite us with her spiritually, so that the Virgin stands in heaven as a mediator of joy and gladness for humankind. To bless the Virgin is then in itself a mysterious means of entry into bliss and glory.

Observations concerning the Virgin's inner life

The Virgin lived in constant hunger for the righteousness of God. She herself revealed this in her prophetic song of praise: "He has filled the hungry with good things, and the rich He has sent away empty." The Virgin here spoke of herself and the eternal blessings to which she gained admittance by virtue of her constant hungering after the righteousness of God.

The Virgin lived constantly in the fear of God. This too is clear from her own words, "His mercy is on those who fear Him from generation to generation." She sensed the greatness of the mercy God had showered on her and immediately perceived that the mercy of God had been hindered in the past because previous generations had not lived in fear of Him. As for her, when she lived in perfect fear of God, she perceived and discerned that mercy was being showered upon her and upon all the coming generations, so she was able to declare decisively, and from experience, that the mercy of God is related to the fear of God.

The Virgin was elevated through her humility to sit upon a throne of honor. Her own words show this too. "He has put down the mighty from their thrones, and exalted those of low degree." The Virgin herself was describing how she was raised up by the hand of the Almighty to sit in her lowliness on a throne of honor in place of the mighty. The Virgin was not boasting of the honor she received; she was proclaiming a certain truth that she knew in her own soul and could only proclaim as good news, as the Holy Spirit had prompted her to declare to the whole human race.

It is therefore not for nothing that the Church believes that the Virgin sits at her Son's right hand. "The queen was set at the King's right hand" (cf. Ps. 45:9). The Virgin herself spoke of this, though in modesty and humility, when she said, referring to herself, "He has put down the mighty from their seats, and exalted those of low degree." And who are the mighty whom God put down from their seats, if not all the kings of former times? And who is the one of low degree whom God exalted and set upon the seats of those kings, if not the Virgin herself?

The Virgin is above the angels

The Apostle Paul tells us that the rank of angel is a rank of service. "The angels are all ministering spirits sent forth to serve, for the sake of those who are to obtain salvation" (Heb. 1:14). And concerning their nature he also says, "Who makes His angels winds, and His servants flames of fire" (Heb. 1:7).

God revealed to us, in His choice of the Virgin to conceive and give birth to the Word the Son of God incarnate of her flesh and blood, how lofty human nature is when its purity returns and it enters into its potential for unity with the divine nature. The purity of the Virgin was able to overcome the disability into which humankind had sunk through sin, and raise up human nature to a status higher than that of the angels, so that she was even able to receive the indwelling of the Word of God in her womb. Even though human nature had been relegated to a state lower than the nature of the angels because of sin and rebellion and the imposition of the curse of death, the Virgin, through her purity, humility, and perfect submission to the will of God, received a promise from God, the Son of the Most High. In her receiving this promise, human nature was elevated, in the Virgin, to a state of glory that made it fit to be the source from which the Son of God should take His body. Thus the Virgin, by the intervention of the Holy Spirit and the power of the Most High, overcame the disability of human nature and was raised up higher than the angels. While the Virgin was carrying the Holy Son of God in her womb, and while she gazed every day into the light of His face, the angels were hiding their faces, as they still do, from the brightness of His glory.

It is therefore not without reason that the tradition of the Church boldly assigns to the Virgin a greater honor than that given the angels and all the archangels, and even the cherubim. Angels, although they are spirits of fire, are still not able to receive the consuming nature of God, but this blessed maid contained in her poor flesh and blood the fiery nature of God, of which the angels stand in awe, and nothing stood in her way because of the great purity and humility she had attained.

The intercession of the Virgin

When the Virgin intercedes for our aid, healing, or repentance, she draws us into the realm of her relationship with Christ. In Orthodoxy, intercession raises us to the level of the intercessor, bringing us into the presence of Christ, then the mediator disappears. This is to say that intercession is a communion with Christ by grace; the Virgin grants us all the powers granted to her so that we might come before Christ. We then stand before Him as the Virgin, that is, in the spirit and grace of purity and holiness granted to us in her. This is what Paul did with all his might: "I betrothed you to Christ to present you as a pure bride to her one husband" (2 Co. 11:2).

This speaks, in the first place, for the correctness of the Orthodox concept of intercession because, in the last analysis, it cancels out the distinction between the intercessor, that is the Virgin, and us. We take from the Virgin the courage that derives from her purity and the audacity that derives from her motherhood and her unique love for Christ. All these things are considered to have been granted to her for our sake, and she, in her great confidence before God, is able to transfer them to us, just as a stronger member in the body grants its strength to a weaker one.

Second, this kind of intercession removes all the barriers between us and Christ. We approach Him unhindered and unimpeded by our weakness, to take from Him help or a particular request or healing or repentance. It is only this that can truly be called intercession. The interceding servant must be prepared to put himself in the place or situation of the servant for whom he intercedes, and must even be prepared to give all he has to make up for the deficiency of his fellow servant.

But intercession can only take place if one is able to step forward in the spirit of the intercessor and be prepared to take or borrow those qualities which make him able to intercede. Otherwise there can be no intercession. The Virgin demonstrates for us the first quality, the essential character required for us to meet with God. Those who deny the role of the Virgin in the incarnation or in intercession, or who deny the importance of purity, do so only in theory, for in practice it is impossible to deny or eliminate them. As far as the incarnation is concerned, God could only be incarnate in purity. As far as intercession is concerned, it is equally impossible for God to reveal Himself or act outside the realm of purity. "Blessed are the pure in heart, for they shall see God" (Mt. 5:8).

The least impurity, even if it be only a passing thought, is enough to hide the face of God, for impurity is darkness and is the work of the devil. It is therefore impossible for one to enter into the presence of God in prayer or meditation if there exists the least inclination to impurity in one's heart, mind, or body. This state of purity can only be attained by intention of the mind in fervent prayer, and by clinging to grace through the blood of Christ. This will immediately procure from God the gift of holiness and the grace of purity for the mind and body.

Intercession requires a personal presence; the Virgin presents herself in the purity before Christ, on our behalf and within the sphere of our experience. In so doing she opens up before us a door that can lead to the spirit of purity and the awakening of a sense of holiness. "The spirits of prophets are subject to prophets" (1 Co. 14:32).

The Virgin Mary represents a human experience that succeeded in plumbing the depths of union with God through a supreme purity that became hers through the Word. She took purity from God and He took from her a body. The Virgin thus became a pattern of union with God, and it remains true that the only quality required of an intercessor is that he surrender what he has.

Blessed is the Virgin, and blessed are those who bless her.

19.

One Christ and One Catholic Church[1]

In an age like ours, tinged as it is with sectarianism, we are apt to think that the words *We believe in one catholic Church* refer to a oneness that applies to the sect or dogma to which a given Christian belongs, whether it be Eastern Orthodox, Roman Catholic, or Protestant. It follows that catholicity is taken as necessarily denoting sectarian unity. An Orthodox believer insists that the oneness of the Church simply lies in its Orthodoxy, catholicity implying only those who are the Orthodox in the world. Such also might be the claim of a Catholic as well as a Protestant. Thus the theological concept of the nature of the Church takes shape for each and every Christian as though its unity were confined to the limits of dogma, and also bounds its catholicity, the latter being presumably a local aspect of the Church.

In such a narrow-minded concept which fanatically adheres to modes of thinking and to parochial perspectives,

[1]Note from the editor of "Vestnik" (No. 133) for the first article by Fr. Matthew in Russian, "One Christ and One Catholic Church":

Fr. Matthew belongs to the Coptic (Egyptian) Church. The non-acceptance of the Chalcedonian definitions, basic for the true faith, by the non-Chalcedonian Churches, was caused to a great extent by misunderstandings in terminology, as well as by a certain apprehension about the imperial designs of Constantinople. At present, however, most scholars agree that no real dogmatic differences exist between the so-called Chalcedonian and non-Chalcedonian (Coptic, Ethiopian, Armenian, and Syriac-Malabarian) Churches—we all believe in Christ the God-Man. To seek full ecclesiastical unity with the non-Chalcedonian Churches is the first and most urgent duty of the Orthodox Church.

what is lost is the reality of the infinite nature of the Church, which transcends the physical earth as well as thought. But the Church is much greater than man! It is even greater than heaven and earth, for man has never filled the Church, nor will he ever be able to do so even if the whole world with all its beliefs and structures were saved (both prospectively and retrospectively speaking). For Christ is the only One who can fill the Church. In Him there abides the entire fullness that can fill all in all, fill man and his mind, fill time and space. The universe with its earth and celestial heavens can by no means contain the Church, yet it is the Church that contains man's heaven and his earth. The Church is the new creation, a new heaven, a new earth, and a new man. In the nature of the new creation, old earth and old heaven are swallowed up, as if they no longer existed, though they actually do. Death is likewise swallowed up into life so that it no longer rules, and the corruptible into the incorruptible as well. All becomes new, alive, everlasting, and pure. Newness, in this respect, pertains to the *unalterable eternal Whole;* oldness is that which inevitably passes away bit by bit because of its essentially mutable nature.

Hence, the Church, with regard to its *catholic* nature is greater than man, his concepts, his structures, and his dogmas, greater even than the universe with its immense heavens, or the vast earth with all its decadence, or temporal events from beginning to end.

The Church is the new Whole. It is from the nature of Christ—out of which has been formed the Church—that this *wholeness* is derived, which includes all that pertains to man and to God through the incarnation.

The Church then is *whole,* in other words *catholic,* as it gathers in its own body of Christ, which fills it, all that belongs to man as well as to God together into one single entity which is both visible and invisible, both finite and infinite, an existence within the sphere of time and place, but at the same time eternal and metaphysical.

The word *catholic* comes from the Greek καθ (in accordance with) and ὅλος (whole). Simply stated, it means "wholeness." The "wholeness" meant here is that which trancsends the totality of finite existence. It is an unalterable, infinite, unbreakable, inumerable whole; it is ONE, a fixed Whole analogous to the concept of Christ's nature which is indivisible, unconfused, and unchangeable.

Such is the Church, which follows Christ in all His aspects. For as Christ is unique in His person, inclusive in His nature, simultaneously whole in His temporal and eternal, His local and universal existence, so is the Church also single and catholic. It follows then that whoever is within the Church is necessarily one and should inevitably be one because of the catholicity of the Church; in other words the Church has the divine capacity attained through Christ to make every single person one with God. Whoever is in Christ is from God and is one with God.

The means the Church uses to practice its catholicity are the sacraments, for through the sacraments all the faithful are brought together into union with the mystical body of Christ, thus becoming one body and one spirit; they have access to the nature of the *one catholic* Church, the body of Christ in the Church being the secret of its catholicty, His person the secret of its oneness.

If the faithful do not achieve a state of single-heartedness and single-mindedness, effected by partaking of the one body and then a state of one love effected by the person of Christ who reigns over all, the sacraments become no more than merely a formal existence, leading to intellectual and dogmatic discord. Sacramental or dogmatic formality is incompatible with the reality of the one comprising body, that which gives life to those who eat of it, and become one in it. In the Church the body of Christ is a source of life and unification; it is both alive and life-giving, and is also capable of abolishing all sorts of barriers created by time and place, as well as by human intellect and instincts, whether it be social barriers ("Neither slave nor freeman in Christ") or racial and cultural barriers ("neither Jew nor Greek, neither barbarian nor Scythian") or sexual barriers ("neither man nor woman" [Ga. 3:28]). The mystical body of Christ in the Church is that source of power which makes it capable of gathering all within its own *unique catholic* nature.

The Church is the new creation; whereas Adam had been the head of the old human creation and the only one from whom all races, peoples, elements, and classes of mankind had sprung, so Christ has become the second Adam and head of the new human creation and the only one from whom the new man has sprung as one chosen race (race here being the divine Christian one) as one justified people (the people here being those who are gathered together by the righteousness of Christ and not by that of its own), and as one holy nation (the only mother here being holy baptism and not a woman's womb). The great secret behind the power of Christ in unifying races and peoples and in abolishing all barriers among all people on earth (ecclesiastical catholicity) lies in His being an incarnate God, the Son of God and the Son of Man simultaneously. The divinity of Christ has caused His humanity to surpass all raciality, nationality, and partiality, even sin and death. Christ's sonship, with respect to God, has enabled Him to gather mankind into a single filiation to God. Hence, whoever partakes of the flesh of Christ has all sorts of barriers dissolved in him together with sin and death. He is thus made one with every man, a new man, newly and purely created in a manner analogous to the image of Christ, a son of God within the unique filiation of Christ. In the Church the *catholic nature* has become dependent on the divine flesh of Christ as implying a power to gather mankind and unify him within a single sonship to God.

Catholicity in the Church is that of Christ; it is the making effective of the nature of Christ which is capable of bringing together simultaneously man with man and man with God. In other words the Church, by nature of its catholicity, is against all sorts of discrimination, division, isolation, and even all that causes division, whatever its source may be, whether within man or outside of him. Christ not only gathers the dispersed colors and races into one mind and one faith, but also gathers them into one flesh in the full sense of the word that implies intimacy, understanding, and love. The Church is His mystical body, with its baptism and its eucharist, the meeting point of all humankind and the only meeting point for all peoples, nations, races, tongues, and colors

which dissolves all barriers and disagreements. Thus all becomes one, great, pure body, one spirit intimate and loving,
one reconciled man whose head is Christ, to whom pertains
all that belongs to races, peoples, colors, and tongues concerning privileges and talents, but void of any division, dispute, or discrimination—which is exactly what is meant by
the "catholicity" of the Church.

The reason is plain and simple why the Church has not
yet achieved its catholicity, or rather why it does not live by
its catholic nature which ought to be the essence of its life in
Christ, the proof of its power, the secret of its wholeness or
divine integrity. It has not yet conceived its divine concepts
as pure and elevated above logic or human reason; i.e. its
concepts are still bound to articulate and philosophical inter-
pretations which hinder the vision of the serenity of the
catholic nature of Christ which has the exquisite power of
total reconciliation and the unification of sundry dispositions
in such a manner that surpasses the capability of any nature
in itself, and not only ideas, principles, and dogmas, being
thus founded upon the forgiveness, purification, justification,
and even the sanctification of every person by the blood of
Christ which is capable of redeeming the sins of the whole
world. It is as if the Church has not yet discovered the depths
of power inherent in the blood of Christ and the working
potentiality of His flesh and the depth of His love and
righteousness.

It is quite obvious that all of the theological terms—as
far as defects are concerned—are in themselves without blemish. The defects have occurred in their interpretation and in
their comprehension; man, here, has approached the divine—
i.e. the simple and serene nature of God—with Adam's mind
and thought, but not with those of Christ. Disagreement here
is an inevitable and necessary obligation of the schismatic
nature of Adam. The schism manifested in comprehending
and perceiving Christ does not lie in Christ's nature, nor does
it belong to His catholic nature, but occurred as a result of
the schism essentially inherent in man's nature, a nature
which has been obliterated by sin and has become full of
hatred, suspicion, misunderstanding, vanity, and disunity. The

fault in the Church's schism lies not in the nature of the
Church, but in the nature of man's ability to conceive and
grasp the nature of Christ and the Church.

Therefore, we can see that any schism in the concept of
the nature of Christ and the Church signals that we have
mundanely approached the divine through a fallen mind, that
is to say, through an undivine approach. Every schism that
has taken place within the Church implies that man has
started to deal with ecclesiastical matters through an ethno-
centric and racialist mind (which disperses), not in an
ecclesiastical or catholic way (which unites).

It is only for the *new* man that Christ will remain unbreakable, indisputable, and without variation; only for the
man who possesses the mind of Christ will the Church remain
one, unique, and catholic to all people, orthodox in every
thought, and void of any sectarianism of division—only for
the new man who has accepted the nature of Christ deep in his
heart. It is only when people renounce their own will that
the sole will of Christ appears, and when they deny their
passions and hatred, curb their bodies and minds to the work
of the Holy Spirit. Only then will the mystical flesh of Christ
be manifested and exert its action in the Church toward the
gathering of hearts, principles, and ideas. When people
earnestly surrender their lives to Christ, only then will the
life of Christ be manifested in the Church, and then will His
Spirit be poured out over it. When every soul within the
Church spiritually, faithfully, and earnestly yields through
fervent repentance to God, and when every Church yields
as such, then will the Church be one through the grace of
God, then will Churches be one through the power of the
Holy Spirit, where Christ becomes one shepherd to the one
flock He rules Himself with His Spirit, thus becoming the
source of its catholicity and its unity.

Is not the Church a manifestation of Christ's incarnation
on earth and His continuity throughout time? In it the faithful form the new human nature, glorified in the person of
Christ, through whom it is adopted by God. How is Christ
to be manifested in the Church, except through the oneness
of thought, will, desire, and sense common among the chil-

dren of the only God who were born not of blood nor of the
will of the flesh nor of the will of man, but through human
and spiritual unity (cf. Jn. 1:13).

How is it going to be proved to the world that God is one,
except through the oneness of those born from Him?

And how is the world to verify that Jesus Christ is the
only begotten Son except through the oneness of the sonship
of those who believe in Him, who are born of God through
His death on their behalf and through His resurrection along
with them, who are now united with His flesh, His blood,
and His Spirit? In other words they have all become members
in one body.

Is it not obvious that the catholicity of the Church and
its oneness are but the totality of theology, the proof of
Christ's existence and action, the actualization of man's new
birth which he obtained from heaven by water and the Holy
Spirit?

The lack of integrity with respect to the catholicity and
unity of the Church, until now, among the Churches of the
world does demand of us—not reconsidering our theology,
for our theology is true and faithful—to reconsider ourselves
in view of our correct theology so that we might correct our
vision of God the only Father of all humankind and correct
our view of Christ as the only Savior and the only Redeemer
of all who call on His name, through whom is indiscriminately
adopted the whole of humanity by God, thus correcting our
love toward man—every person—as being inevitably a brother
to us, even if he stood against us in hostility and set forth for
us snares of death.

Yet it should be borne in mind that what urges us to
attain such ecclesiastical catholicity and unity is not merely
theological zeal or idealism or even remorse; it should be out
of our own faith, our own love, that is to say out of the newness of our new birth which is from heaven and which can by
no means be made effectual to us. We cannot abide in it
apart from the catholicity of the Church and its unity.

The new man can never live separate from others or as a
broken part or with hatred or hostility against others. The
new man must be *whole* and *one,* for it is out of one catholic

nature and one Father that he emerges. The one new nature with which every man in the Church is born is that which makes *one* of the *whole* through grace and spirit. Love here imposes its divine and catholic authority. Into the image of Christ the only begotten Son are baptized all those born to the Father by the only paternity.

The Church thus is catholic because it is the body of the Son (sacrificed for the whole world through love), who recapitulates all things within Himself. The Church is one because it is the unbreakable house of the Father.

We now look forward most eagerly with tears and supplication, with the new man's consciousness, to the Church's catholicity and to its unity all over the world.

20.

Christian Unity

*Holy Father, who hast glorified Thy Son Jesus and hast
conferred upon Him power over all flesh, so that He may
grant eternal life to all those who have believed in Him,
God and Savior; we give Thee thanks that Thou hast vouch-
safed unto us men to know the consubstantial unity between
Thee, Thy Son, and Thy Holy Spirit to which Thou hast called
us by the prayer that Thy Son made unto Thee: "That they
may all be one; even as Thou, Father, art in Me, and I in Thee,
that they also may be one in us, so that the world may believe
that Thou hast sent Me" (Jn. 17:21).*

*Indeed we believe that the unity to which Thou hast
called us is necessary for the witness of the mystery of Thy
work in human nature, a nature prone to corruption and dis-
integration because of sin and selfishness. Likewise, this unity
is necessary that the world may believe that it has no other
hope but in the person of Jesus Christ, Thy dearly beloved
Son, whom Thou hast sent to join the things of heaven with
the body.*

*We acknowledge and confess that the advent of Thy Son
in our hearts ("that Christ may dwell in your hearts through
faith" [Eph. 3:17]) must create in us an immediate drawing
towards unity: "I in them, and Thou in me, so that they may
become perfectly one, so that the world may know that Thou
hast sent Me and hast loved them ever as Thou hast loved Me
(Jn. 17:23). It follows, therefore, that any opposition on our
part to the perfection of unity in Thee, a unity which Thou
hast sought for us, is in us weakness of faith and lack of*

*charity. These shortcomings cause us to place ideological,
political, and racial controversies above the demands of conscience, faith, and love, and cause us to stifle the voice of
Christ in our hearts, in order to satisfy the world and man.*

*Holy Father, glorify Thy Son in the life of Thy Church,
so that the Church may glorify Thee and glorify Thy Son,
when all have rid themselves of everything that hinders unity
and hampers charity. Permit it not, O Lord, that Thy people
should cease from being, and try to remove sin by means that
are themselves sinful, or to cure evil by another evil; permit
it not that unity should be sought through differences of
opinion, charity confounded with politics, and racial align-
ments considered as a spiritual force.*

Christian unity

It is because the Christian seeks God that he seeks unity; he
feels it present in his soul, according to the measure in which he
feels the presence of God. Christian unity is, therefore, a
supreme demand of faith; we seek it because it is entreating
us from the bottom of our hearts. Yet, since all do not have
the same awareness of God, unity is not approached from the
same angle; it expands or contracts within men in proportion
to their hearts' relationship with God. Some do not feel it at
all; others even deny it. It is a test of faith.

The principle of theological unity springs initially from
a maturity of faith and from an overflowing spirituality
which bursts through the barriers of hate, the variance of
thought, the discords of the soul, the inventions of the intellect, and the cares of the flesh. The unity of men is an ideal
that surpasses human strength if it is sought at a divine
level. It flows, as a *necessity*, as an *inevitable* and direct
consequence, from the union of man with God. This is a
well-known law of spirituality, based as much on practical
experience as on the repeated witness of Scripture. The first
commandment says, "You shall love the Lord your God with
all your heart, and with all your soul, and with all your
mind," and the second: "You shall love your neighbor as

yourself" (Mt. 22:37-39). Scripture affirms here that the second commandment springs from the first. It is from the first that it proceeds. The second without the first would have no value; it would indeed be near to sin.

Therefore, the insistence that is put on the demand for unity at the present time, when different Churches are complaining of flagging faith in their clergy and their laity and of spiritual weakness and the refusal of the young to consecrate their lives to the Lord, leads us to set out ideas in order. What can be the driving force which has led this insistence on unity to take such a pervasive form?

If there were indeed a spiritual renaissance, a deep fervor for the faith, unity would have taken the form of a collective and individual return to God, a sweeping movement for conversion, repentance, and begging God for forgiveness—as has always happened to God's people after a period of half-heartedness or aberration. But so insistent a search for unity at a moment when we are in such a state of altering lukewarmness, when we are openly practicing separation and withdrawal from God, leads us to ask: where does this urge come from?

Man originally came from a single being, Adam. It is normal, therefore, that there should be within people an instinctive longing for friendship, a longing unconsciously nourished by our instinctive feelings.

On the other hand, since we live in the same world, our interests are sometimes brought into harmony, but at other times are in such conflict that life itself and existence are affected; hence another longing, a longing for a fellowship opposed to the hostile elements, a fellowship in which man unites against man.

Unity based on the emotional approach

It would be an extremely serious matter to misunderstand emotion and to allow it to penetrate and permeate our quest for Christian unity, which must be sought through the Spirit without any interference from the flesh or from emotion:

"That which is born of the flesh is flesh; and that which is born of the Spirit is spirit" (Jn. 3:6). Satisfaction of the emotions, even if it appears just and beautiful, especially in matters of the spirit, is incapable of answering the demands of truth, for truth, in the final count, cancels emotion: "Those who are in the flesh cannot please God (Rm. 8:8). Thus emotion, even if it appears to be in accord with the spirit at the start of the road leading to truth, nevertheless represents a danger capable of blocking our way and turning us back from the ascent. Emotion, therefore, works unconsciously for the benefit of the flesh; even if it submits itself to the spirit, it is only a ruse to clothe itself in spiritual qualities and to exploit them for the benefit of personal glorification.

If the unity of men—under a spiritual guise—bases itself on emotion, it can only serve the glorification of what is human, the exaltation of the human "me." God, in the process, becomes merely secondary. Deliberations and negotiations then become a sort of attempt—a serious one—to discover a common language that may be used for the mutual understanding of the "men of Babel," so as to undertake once more the erection of the tower leading to heaven.

The "me" is indeed the source of the division that reigns throughout the entire world, and in a special way within the Church.

God demands unity among men so that *He* may be the head: "That they may be [one] in us" (Jn. 17:21). Divine unity among men, therefore, is equivalent to stripping man of the individual and the collective "me."

Emotion is the most deceptive form of "me" because it is closest to the spirit. Whether my emotion deceives me or whether it deceives the other party who for his "self" wishes to form a union with me is neither here nor there; it is possible to renounce the "me" in order that another may be exalted instead of God. In this case my renunciation would be nothing but an illusion, for I ought, in the first place, to have made a complete renunciation of the "me" and all my emotions in the presence of God, *before* trying to unite myself with others. According to the order of progression taught by the Scriptures, I should have to have loved God "with *all* my heart, and with *all* my soul, and with *all* my mind" so as to be able to love others with a unifying love that cannot bring harm to me or to them.

Union is not an emotional surrender but rather an ascent free of personal feelings, an ascent which one does not accomplish by oneself nor through oneself; it is a magnetic pull, rather than an effort, to encounter each other in the presence of God and not just in the presence of one another: "No man can come to Me, unless the Father who sent Me draws him (Jn. 6:44).

The road to union with God is not a one-way street ending solely with God; on the return journey it leads back to one's neighbor, the stranger, one's enemy, and toward all creation. He who unites himself to God undertakes to consider how he should unite himself to all and takes no rest until that union has been accomplished. This road that leads to God and from Him is found within man.

If, therefore, Christian unity is not realized at the present time, it is: (a) because we are seeking it before we have surrendered our whole heart and our whole soul and our whole mind to God, and (b) because we are seeking it outside ourselves; that is to say, we are trying to realize it as a matter for discussion and not within ourselves.

To seek unity before arriving at a state of complete abandonment of heart and soul and mind to God is to enter either into an emotional conflict, so that we seek unity for our own sake, or else into an intellectual illusion, seeking unity for its own sake as an exigency which the logic of faith necessitates. The intellect, let us not forget, is a force which emotion exploits—until we reach the state of total abandonment to God.

To seek unity outside oneself is to deviate into matters of interest and speculation. Interesting discussion always gives rise to opposing points of view and insoluble discord; the subject is considered from different angles, each person having his own perspective which is the true one for him, but is certainly not so to others.

Unity is not a subject that can ever be examined theoretically; unity is initially a divine essence and consequently a truth. But divine truth has neither angles or "variation, or shadow due to change (Jm. 1:17). It is seen by everyone in its totality in a single flash, for it is simple. One cannot see it outside God or without him, for he who sees the attributes of God, of necessity sees God: "He who has seen me has seen the Father" (Jn. 14:9).[1] God said: "I will make all my goodness pass before thee (Ex. 33:19). It is said that Moses saw God "face to face" (Ex. 33:11), although he had only seen the goodness of God.

God inhabits the heart and manifests Himself there; the heart[2] is filled with the attributes of God and comprehends unity in its depth and in its truth.

Unity is one of the desires of God that Christ revealed to us: "That they may be [one] in us" (Jn. 17:21). It is, therefore, within ourselves that it is to be sought and studied —if, of course, Christ is in fact within our heart ("that Christ may dwell in your hearts through faith [Eph. 3:17]).

Today unity is a subject sought in every field *to prepare* for the union of all with God. This is nothing but an illusion: unity cannot be "temporarily" separated from God so as to be a means of access to God. Unity will become a living fact when all are in God.

The search for unity is now conducted along lines that are based on reason and at the same time exposed to the ebb and flow of emotion; it is a sort of "spiritualized" scientific research. Now, unity is not a science, it is not subject to the development of knowledge based on the distinction between correct and incorrect, between good and bad. Unity is truth and truth inspires and inspiration lodges itself first in the heart and only then in the understanding: "Did not our *heart* burn within us while He talked?" "And their eyes were opened and they recognized Him" (Lk. 24:31f). This order of progression appears even more clearly in the Epistle to the

[1]The quotation in this context implies the divine qualities manifested by the Son of God in a humble appearance of the Son of Man. (Note from the Russian translation.)

[2]In the ascetic and mystical theology of the Christian East (as in the Bible) "heart" means not merely the seat of the emotions and affections, but also the primary center of man's being, man considered as a spiritual subject. (Note from an English version.)

Hebrews: "This is the covenant that I will make with them after those days, says the Lord; I will put my laws on their hearts and write them on their minds" (Heb. 10:16).

Inspiration never neglects reason, but reason always lacks inspiration. We do not want to neglect the search for unity on the intellectual plane, for the mind points out human failings and then passes judgment on them; that is its function, and its concern with analysis is profitable for a little.[3] But unity is an edification of the soul, the gathering together of its powers. This is the concern of the spirit: the spirit forgives and pardons, loves and unites.

Unity surpasses the capacity of the mind. All that reason could do would be to understand it once it had been accomplished, but it could not grasp beforehand how it would be accomplished: "the Kingdom of God is not coming with signs to be observed" (Lk. 17:20).

The union of men in some town or other at one end of the earth, then in another at the other end, is a good thing, for indeed it is just this which is truly preparing for the divine presence, if it is based on the willingness of each one to receive the divine presence and is not simply a gathering together of the community.

If we desire a true unity, we must seek it and study it in God, in His presence, not as some theoretical subject separated from God, whatever theological guise it may adopt.

In the presence of God, human understanding adopts an attitude of "response" to the divine presence, not one of "proposal." This attitude of response is the result of stronger, more intense reactions in the heart, reactions echoing the inspiration that always accompanies the divine presence.

It is therefore within the person that unity is studied, and it is discerned through the divine presence and through finding that presence.

Unity without the divine presence is nothing more than an idea, a matter for discussion, or a vain longing. But in the presence of God unity becomes real and visible, overflowing and life-giving, and many live it. When Christ is present in

---

[3] Just as "bodily training is of some value" (1 Tm. 4:8). (Note from a French version.)

the midst of a community in conflict, controversy cannot keep
from ceasing. Every member must begin to fill his eyes and
his heart with true unity, and prepare his whole being to
receive unity and to give it.

Any question concerning unity on the theological plane
which cannot find a solution is indeed sufficient proof that
the Lord is not present in the midst of the assembly. The
Lord's absence necessarily causes one to think again about
the aim of the union, the method of seeking it, and the intention of its united members.

It is certain that, should we divest ourselves of our individual "me" and our ecclesial "me," as much on the conscious
as on the subconscious level, unity would without question
become a reality.

It is impossible to rid oneself of the "me" in all its
aspects, traditional, logical, canonical, and sacred; the individual is incapable of detaching himself from it, however
great his control over himself may be. Even if he were repre-
senting his own Church, he would still be incapable of abandoning the "me" of that Church.

But when the Lord is truly and factually present, all existence of "self" vanishes and Christ becomes the "me of all."

In this way, therefore, a man will not make any concessions to his brother, nor will the Churches make any mutual
concessions to each other, but they will all surrender everything to God, just as everything must necessarily be subjected at the end of time: "When all things are subjected to Him then the Son Himself will also be subjected
to Him who put all things under Him, that God may be
everything to everyone" (1 Co. 15:28).

The question in the matter of unity is in a penetrating and
decisive manner the question of the presence of the Lord; it
is by this presence that unity will be accomplished, on the
divine plane, and that divisions will be brought to an end.

The Lord alone can make both one, and break down the
middle wall of partition (cf. Eph. 2:14).

This question has two aspects, unity and the removal of
differences on the level of the two commandments: first "You
shall love the Lord your God," and second "You shall love

your neighbor" (Mt. 22:37-39). Human logic would like us first to remove the differences so unity could be accomplished, whereas the logic of God, as it is expressed in the inspiration of the second chapter of the Epistle to the Ephesians, requires that unity should be accompilshed first, so that the middle partition may be broken down.

This is the mutual opposition that exists at the present time in meetings on Christian unity. The necessity forces itself upon us of once more paying attention to the problem of unity, so it can exist according to the way of God.

Unity based on the trend toward union on the natural level

Unity is the fusion of the one *into* the other, to put an end to the many; therefore, in outward appearance unity is weakness, but in essence it is an immense force, as indivisible as God.

"Union," on the other hand, consists of joining the one *to* the other so that they may become many; therefore, in outward form "union" is a movement toward force or domination, but in essence it is weakness, complete weakness, for it carries the meaning of impotence and fear.

There is a danger that Christian unity could be made to exist out of the instinct for natural union, whether it stems from the weak in order to gain strength, or from the powerful in order to increase power. In either case it would be to pursue the temporal life, and that would be incompatible with the practice of Christian life: "Do not fear those who kill the body" (Lk. 12:4).

The strength of Christian life comes neither from the many nor from "union," but from union with God: "for [it] is God at work in you, both to will and to work for His good pleasure" (Ph. 2:13).

To propose Christian unity to a weak Church that is exposed to injustice, persecution, or poverty is to subject it to a dangerous temptation, to rouse its subconscious to preserve "union" in order to face up to the danger that is disturbing it. Then it becomes extremely difficult for that Church to distinguish in its thinking between the divine unity demanded by God and the unity of the many demanded by the instinct of self-preservation. That is why any proposal of Christian unity to a Church exposed to hostile factors represents for its conscience a trial a thousand times harder than the persecution it already is suffering.

For that Church—oppressed by persecution—to choose Christian unity, acting on a free choice and not to escape from bitter facts, it would have to show enlightened discernment, prudence, mortification, and total surrender to God. What is more, all this is not enough if, before examining the possibility of unity, it had not reached acceptance of the bitter facts to the point of being ready to persevere in them even to the last of its faithful adherents.

At this point the yearning for unity, and its motives, will indeed spring from the state of divine life of that Church, and will proceed to it from God Himself through His inspiration, instead of being instigated by the bitter circumstances in which the Church finds itself or being dictated by instinctive opposition to hostile forces.

In order for us to secure for the weak and persecuted Churches the true meaning of "Christian unity" in their journey through history and in their encounters with temporal situations, and in order for the divine consciousness to rise in them, the first necessity is that they should understand that Christian unity is a state of *divine weakness over against the world*—like that of their Master, who surrendered His infinite power to be crucified by anyone who wished and in whatever way they wished.

Christ, desiring to reveal to us "the strength of His weakness"—if one may so describe it—drew His disciples' attention to it at the very moment of His testing, although He was being subjected to the most appalling trials that a defenseless man could endure: "Do you think that I cannot appeal to my Father, and He will at once send me more than twelve legions of angels?" (Mt. 26:53). What prevented the Lord from having an escort like this? To be crucified while being surrounded by twelve legions of angels—was this possible?

Behind the "escort" of Christian unity there lurks a human

danger that threatens its "weakness"—if one may put it this way. The unity of Christian Churches misleads the ailing conscience into believing that its Christian state and temporal strength are guaranteed, when in fact the temporal weakness of the Church is its most precious possession; it is its glory and its strength, for it is "divine weakness." Or, as the Apostle Paul said, "the weakness of God is stronger than men" (1 Co. 1:25).

The Church that has temporal power cannot taste a crucifixion that is forced upon it, for one cannot be crucified except through weakness, like the Master of all, who "was crucified in weakness" (2 Co. 13:4).

For Churches that are powerful in the temporal sense, or that are supported by the powers of this age, the prospect of Christian unity represents the temptation of falling into a tangle of emotion and exultation, adopting the role of "liberator" just as Pilate may have done when, sitting on the judgment seat and having before him the Lord chained and clothed in the robe of mockery, said, "You will not speak to me? Do you not know that I have power to release you?" (Jn. 19:10).

A man's coming down from the cross in no way proves that he is a son of God. He who believes that he can bring another down from the cross assuredly proves that he does not understand the "will of the Father." Temporal weakness necessitates the cross. The cross in our life is a foundation; the cross is "the *power* of God for salvation . . ." (Rm. 1:16) and His "power is made perfect in weakness" (2 Co. 12:9). With our free will we pray for weakness, and we bear it without fear if it comes to us, for with weakness there is always grace: "My grace is sufficient for you for my power is made perfect in weakness" (2 Co. 12:9).

Renunciation of the instinct for "union" was exercised by the Lord before the crucifixion, in a manner that was both involuntary and voluntary, as it is with all the Lord's actions: "Then all the disciples forsook Him, and fled" (Mt. 26:56); "If you seek me, let these men go" (Jn. 18:8).

The Lord was making a mockery of power when He said to His disciples: "[He] who has no sword [let him] sell his mantle and buy one" (Lk. 22:36). Power *denudes* man of the power of the Spirit. One cannot at one and the same time put on Christ and put on the world. When Peter decided to bear the sword and use force, he divested himself of grace and he denied with his tongue the very person he wanted to defend with his sword.

When Peter took up the sword with the intention of killing, the Spirit left him and the devil entered in and struck him with the sword of denial and blasphemy; thus was accomplished the word of the Lord to him: "All who take the sword will perish with the sword" (Mt. 26:52). The Lord was only talking of spiritual peril, about which He had already said to Peter: "I have prayed for you that your faith may fail" (Lk. 22:32).

If Christian unity is allied to the idea of temporal force, even if it is only to safeguard the interests of the weak, or if it seems useful for *bringing human pressure to bear* on the wayward sheep, it immediately loses its divine value; it is then nothing but a number of "unions," destined to disintegrate and then to disappear like every temporal undertaking in the works of humanity.

We wish and we pray that the Churches may have a unity, divine both in appearance and in essence, a unity above the realm of time.